Momentum
the hidden **force** *in*
TENNIS

Alistair Higham

Co-published by 1st4sport Publications, an imprint of Coachwise Ltd
Units 2/3 Chelsea Close
Amberley Road
Armley
Leeds LS12 4HW and
Meyer and Meyer Sport (UK) Ltd
Aachen, Olten (CH), Vienna, Québec, Lansing/Michigan, Adelaide, Auckland, Johannesburg

www.1st4sport.com
www.meyer-meyer-sports.com

ISBN: 1-84126-040-1

A CIP catalogue record for this book is available from the British Library.

Editor: Anne Simpkin
Design and Typesetting: Natalie Schmidt
Printed by: Duffield Printers, Leeds

Acknowledgements

Front cover, title page, and foreword photographs: Action Plus

Inside photographs: Action Plus (Pages 1, 3, 11, 15, 31, 38, 49, 54, 57, 67, 71, 84) All other photographs courtesy of Charles Coldwell

Many friends, colleagues and players, too numerous to mention, have played a part in the discussions and ideas that form the basis for *Momentum: The Hidden Force in Tennis*.

I wish to thank, in particular, the following for their specific support, encouragement and, in some cases, critical comment on the material for this book as it has developed over the past six years: Rob Antoun; Rod Blow; Derek Bone; Ashley Broomhead; Jane Carter; Ron Carter; Pamela Cocker; Charles Coldwell; Mark Cox; Penny Crisfield; Paul Dent; Jo Durie; David Felgate; Patrice Hagelauer; Dr Chris Harwood; Joanne Higham; John Higham; Julie Higham; Andrew Jarrett; Alan Jones; Simon Jones; James Lenton; Richard Lewis; Ellinore Lightbody; Anne Pankhurst; Jane Poynder; Mark Rayers; Keith Reynolds; Jane Rushby; Anne Simpkin; Biljana Veselinovic; Martin Weston.

Front Cover: Tim Henman
Serena Williams (Insert)

Title page: A joyful Andre Agassi wins the French Open

Contents

Foreword

Watching a world class tennis match is an opportunity not to be missed. Whether you come to competition tennis from a top club or the park you can recognise Alistair Higham's momentum ideas in the swing of any match. Championship tennis is harnessed momentum at its best.

If you want to improve your match play at whatever level – club matches, county matches, international tournaments, or simply with your friends, this book is a vital tool.

There are many excellent tennis books on where and how to hit your shots, how to focus your mind, and how to get physically fit for tennis matches. They mainly concentrate on improving your skills to improve your tennis – better strokes, better tactics, better concentration, better movement.

Unlike other tennis books, *Momentum: The Hidden Force in Tennis* is about the battle of competitive tennis matches – the ebbs and flows, the turning points, why momentum switches and how and when to use your skills to gain control. It is also an enjoyable read, both thought provoking and original.

Reading through the examples from real matches Alistair has witnessed, I found myself thinking of many similar examples that I had experienced or witnessed throughout my career as a player and a coach.

If you are brushing up your skills or honing your matchplay then you need to measure the momentum too – Good Luck!

David Felgate
International Coach on the ATP Tour

Chapter One

Introducing Momentum

'WHAT IS GOING ON?' shrieked Julia and smashed her racket down. Nothing was working now, and didn't look likely to work. Things had swung against her.

Until 6–1 4–2, it had been plain sailing. Winners came with ease, she was calm and in control while her opponent looked to be giving up. She was coasting home. She couldn't do anything wrong and her opponent couldn't seem to do anything right.

But that was 25 minutes earlier and now it was 6–1 4–6 1–5. All hope of winning had almost gone. Her mind was in turmoil, frustration was building – this match should have been hers.

Then, with a last dying kick, she got angry, hit out and saved three match points at 1–5, another one at 2–5 and suddenly things turned again. Five minutes later, at 5–5 there was only one winner. She won 7–5 in the final set.

This was an international match against Russia in the European Team Championships but it could equally have been a club match, or a friendly match in a park somewhere.

Why do matches twist and turn like this? Why are they so unpredictable?

The answer lies in momentum and its flow. At the end of the match, the result is not always a reflection of the physical skill of the players. It is often a reflection of how the players dealt mentally with momentum being with them or against them – and how they reacted to the situations that can cause a swing in momentum.

This book is about the flow of momentum in tennis. It explains why momentum fluctuates, how you can control it and how to make it work in your favour. The book is not about technique; instead it covers the real problems that tennis players face:

- *How to hold on to a lead.*
- *How to fight back from hopeless positions.*
- *How to grasp opportunities that come your way.*

Before these problems can be solved, we need to know more about momentum itself and how to control it.

Some Key Questions

What is momentum?

Momentum is the force that controls the flow of the match. It is a hidden force. It is invisible because it comes from the flow of energy between competitors. You can sense it when competing or spectating. It dictates the *run of play* – you can *feel* things going for or against you or the players you are watching.

Many words and phrases used in sport are linked to the *flow of momentum*. For example:

- *things are going your way*
- *stepping up a gear*
- *things turning against you*
- *lulled into a sense of false security*
- *holding it together*
- *can't do anything wrong at the moment*
- *things going from bad to worse*
- *took the wind out of your sails*
- *being up against it*
- *plain sailing*
- *having your back to the wall*
- *ebb and flow*
- *turned the tables.*

Momentum exists in all sports and is what makes them so exciting to play and watch. It is why the score does not always reflect the state of play and why the better/stronger player does not always win. Momentum gives sport unpredictability, which is why spectators stay interested.

How does it work?

Momentum acts like water – flowing backwards and forwards, sometimes faster or slower, or at times not moving at all.

The flow of momentum is more than just a sporting phenomenon, it is a fact of life and exists in everything we do. For example, you can look back and see how things went during the course of a meeting, a day at home, a week, a relationship or a career. Once you start thinking in terms of momentum, you can identify where, when and often why things went for or against you. You can spot turning points in your career, your relationship or your game. Of course, like most things, momentum is easier to see in retrospect.

Is momentum controllable?

You'll often hear people say it isn't. In a recent television programme a darts commentator spoke of 'momentum creeping in and creeping out of the match' – as if it had a mind of its own and was not something that might be controlled.

If this is the case, how is it that some players always seem to manage to get momentum on their side when it matters most? It is not random. It is not simply a case of certain players continuing to get lucky, like gamblers on a winning streak. If it were random then the law of averages suggests that simply being strong enough, fast enough or agile enough would ensure sporting success. We know this is not true.

There are certain players who keep winning key points, who know when it matters to win a point or string a series of points together, and who can tell how and when to take action. They seem to possess an ability to perceive such things and to time their moves so that the momentum flows with them.

The flow of momentum can be controlled, just as rivers can be controlled. Momentum can be harnessed and turned to your advantage providing you can identify and use the flow of momentum in the present.

How can you learn to use it?

Through experiencing or reading about practical examples of tennis match play (as given in this book), you can begin to discover what it feels like when the momentum is for you, against you and neutral; how and why momentum switches; how to respond to turning points; and how to establish it, keep it with you or regain it. You will understand why fighting spirit is the key and more importantly, the most effective times to use it.

This book does not just cover raising your general standard of tennis; it focuses on raising your overall standard of competing. Controlling momentum flow is a vital skill for players at any level.

Why is managing momentum important?

There are many factors involved in tennis matches so no two matches appear to be the same. This is because there are so many variables, for example:

- *surfaces*
- *weather conditions*
- *locations*
- *equipment*
- *styles of opponent*
- *mental approaches*
- *form at different times.*

However, if you are a player you will have had the feeling of history repeating itself in seemingly very different situations. This is because momentum is the *secret* link between matches.

Managing momentum will help you bring together and control many of the variable factors that affect you during matches. This book explains why different match situations can produce the same feelings in a player. It helps you to make the most of whatever situations you find yourself in, whether you have just lost four games in a row or need to hold serve in order to win a match.

Greg Rusedski's serve – a bigger weapon on a grass court

How do you know when momentum is with you?

- You feel in control.
- You are relaxed but your mind and senses are sharp.
- Your strokes are smooth and you seem to be doing everything without any real effort.
- You move to the ball easily.
- Lucky things seem to happen.
- The ball and the court seem big.
- You time the ball with ease.
- You do not worry about losing points.
- You have a sense of inevitability about winning.

How do you know when momentum is against you?

- You feel unsettled.
- Nothing seems to be working.
- Your opponent is controlling things even though you are still trying hard.
- Your legs feel leaden and your movements don't flow.
- Your mind is in turmoil trying to find a way out.
- Unlucky things seem to happen.
- The ball and the court seem small.
- You mistime the ball.
- Small things get on your nerves.

Why is momentum hidden?

The first place to see who has the momentum flow *should* be the score, but **momentum does not always follow the score** and the score does not always reflect the past momentum.

This is because a match is a dynamic thing – like a moving picture – and the score on the scoreboard is more like a snapshot. For example, it can be three games all in the final set, which would suggest things are fairly equal. However, like a picture taken of two people *neck and neck* in a race, it can look very different when you know who has the momentum. For instance, the score does not reflect:

- *who has missed chances*
- *who is getting pumped up*
- *who is getting tired*
- *who is starting to play better*
- *who has been riding their luck*
- *whose head is starting to go down*
- *who is just beginning to work out the tactics to win*
- *who has just broken a string in their favourite racket!*

Although it may not be reflected in the score, both players and spectators know with whom the momentum lies. You can sense when a player, who may have lost twice as many games as their opponent, has just gained the *upper hand.*

As it is a hidden force people can come to some common or misguided conclusions about how momentum affects a match behind the headline score, for example: 'he must have got injured' or 'she must have played badly.' Many players underestimate its impact and believe the scoring system will favour the player with a higher standard of play. These people often say 'I should have won, I was the better player'.

Momentum may be hidden behind the scoring system, but it does exist. You can learn to recognise it and how to control it – so the **final** score ends up reflecting that **you** were the better competitor!

Key points:

- Momentum is what you can feel when things go for or against you.
- Controlling the flow of momentum is a vital skill for players at any level.
- Momentum is a hidden force that is there every time we play.
- Beware! The score does not always reflect the flow of a match.

Working with Momentum Flow

Momentum and turning points

If we know that momentum exists ... and we know what it feels like when it's with us and when it's against us ... and we know that it can change hands during a match ... then the key question is: when does it change and why?

When does it change?

The answer became clear to me after years of listening to tennis parents talk about the matches their children had just played.

After matches, while I was talking to the parents about game plans going well or too many unforced errors on the forehand etc, they were talking to me about things that happened during the match, some of which didn't seem to be related to the tennis at all.

They'd say things like: 'Everything was going badly at first, but she picked up when her best friend came to play her match on the next court. It gave her just the boost she needed'. Or 'He was going well until he broke a string in his favourite racket'.

As a trained tennis coach, I thought these parents were missing the point so I would simply listen politely, then go off to calculate the percentage of missed first serves.

However, they were picking up things that I was missing. As supporters, they sensed when things were going well and badly, and why they changed. They may not have been experts in tennis strategy, but they were experts in spotting their children's mental reactions to certain situations and the effect these had on the match.

What they were describing were **turning points** in the momentum flow.

Turning points (see panel on the following page) are usually unpredictable. They can produce momentum shifts and affect the flow of the match. They are always related to one of three things:

- *The actions of your opponent.*

- *Your own actions.*

- *External events that affect one or both of you.*

Examples of turning points include:

- *bad line calls*
- *net cord for or against you*
- *broken strings*
- *change in the weather*
- *biased clapping from opponent's supporters*
- *coach coming to watch*
- *coach leaving*
- *girlfriend/boyfriend arriving/leaving*
- *change of court surface due to the weather*
- *opponent's time-out due to illness or injury*
- *blisters*
- *opponent starts to limp or show visible signs of illness, but only in between the points*
- *winning/losing a long game*
- *gamesmanship*
- *opponent changing tactics*
- *warning from the umpire*
- *toilet breaks*
- *losing a close set*
- *missing an easy shot*
- *breaking a racket in anger*
- *poor ball boys/girls*
- *players arguing on the next court.*

Why does it change?

Turning points all have one thing in common: they have the potential to **cause a change in the balance of the mental energy** of one player or the other, which then causes a change in the momentum flow of the match. Turning points can happen when a player's mental energy is boosted by something or, more often, when a player is distracted by something. The bigger the change, the faster the momentum can swing.

Some turning points are predictable. Others can come from the most unlikely sources, some of which will apparently have little to do with tennis (eg a player worrying about whether they will finish in time to watch the football!). The one certainty is that potential turning points will happen in *every* match.

Turning points, however, are only *potential* turning points. They will end up either as a turning point or merely a blip depending on your response to what happens. For example, if you miss a smash on match point, but regain your composure and concentration immediately, the match probably won't turn around. On the other hand, if you panic, change your game plan (eg start trying to hit clean winners to win quickly), the flow of the match could turn against you. In other words, **it's not what goes wrong that's important, but your response to what goes wrong.**

Luck and turning points

Luck, of course, can play a big role in turning points. Not everything is controllable. At key times, a lucky shot can happen but it is fairly rare (and rarely fair!). Some people put too much down to luck and are always claiming to be unlucky. For example, they will make excuses such as:

* *'my string broke'*

* *'I just ran out of steam in the third set'*

* *'my opponent kept hitting passing shot winners on the big points'.*

Of course they wouldn't say this if they had had enough well strung rackets, were fit enough and knew on which side to approach!

If you respect luck and have the right reaction to it, you will find that there is some truth to the phrase: *You make your own luck.*

However, luck will still play its part so have a positive attitude towards it. When you are lucky, be thankful and make sure you examine your tactics carefully, because you might not be able to rely on luck again. When you are unlucky, renew your efforts and bounce back straight away. After all, you don't remember lucky shots against you when you win.

Becoming a tennis expert

Tennis experts are those who are tuned into momentum and its swings. They realise that a match is a moving picture and don't get too excited when momentum goes in their favour or too depressed when it is against them. This is because they know it can, and does, shift. They are able to appreciate that an extra effort may well be needed at certain points. They are also ready for their opponent to make an extra effort at certain points.

Tennis experts are not necessarily those who play the game at a professional level. Everyone can improve the way they play and the results they achieve by becoming more of a tennis expert. Everyone can improve their tennis by becoming more expert in the flow of the match because momentum exists at all standards.

Key points:

- A shift in momentum is often traced back to a particular point or event (ie a turning point).

- Turning points are created by the actions of players or external events. They can be merely *a blip* if players regain their composure immediately.

- You can make luck work for or against you!

Chapter Two

Identifying and Controlling Momentum

The Five Stages of Momentum

When you are playing tennis, particularly in the heat of battle, it may well seem that there is no real link between the flow of the match and previous matches you have played. Yet when we look at tennis matches more closely, it is possible to see that the same things happen again and again.

In all kinds of different circumstances, comebacks are being made, leads are being lost, and close fought battles are taking place on tennis courts around the world involving young beginners, club hackers and professional players.

Even though the circumstances are very different, from the players' and spectators' points of view, what links them together are five basic situations – I call them *stages of momentum*. The following five basic stages of momentum apply in all matches, but they do not necessarily relate to the score on the scoreboard:

- When momentum is ***totally with you***
- When momentum is ***with you***
- When momentum is ***neutral***
- When momentum is ***against you***
- When momentum is ***totally against you***

In matches, the flow of momentum moves through these stages sometimes in a straight line, sometimes in a twisting line which turns back on itself. It can move very quickly through the stages if something significant happens or slowly if nothing significant happens. Either way, it seems to be in momentum's nature to want to move, especially if players are of a similar level. Given a bit of encouragement by either player, momentum will shift.

The good news is that it is always in one of the five stages and if you learn how to react to each situation, you will be able to have a big say in which way it moves or even if it moves at all. **Having this knowledge is like having a compass and a map that you can apply to any match and any situation, no matter how different they are.**

The more difficult news is that when you have this map of momentum flow, you will need to have *the right attitude* and fighting spirit in order to control the direction you move.

Let's take a closer look at these five stages and how to control each of them.

When Momentum is Totally With You

When things are going totally for you, it is *plain sailing* – you can afford to relax a little because you have room to allow for it. Even if a few things go wrong, so much has gone right so far, that you can afford it. Everything will be fine, you are certain to win sooner or later.

Can you hear some alarm bells ringing? Me too.

There is some truth in this of course. When things are totally with you: you are in control, you feel confident because you are able to do most of the things you try, and your shots and movements take less effort. In addition, your opponent may well be frustrated and is probably showing signs of it. Indeed, later we will see how you can even try a bit of gambling, but first a word of warning.

If your opponent is of a similar standard, it's very possible that the momentum may swing back in their favour. Occasionally this can happen in a dramatic way after a particular turning point, but more often when the flow is heavily in one direction, it shifts more gradually, gathering more pace as it moves.

This *creeping* change can be averted if you:

- *avoid the dangers*
- *understand the scoring system (it isn't football)*
- *know how you got there*
- *prepare to fight*
- *win the first point*
- *watch for a change in tactics*
- *step up a gear.*

Avoid the dangers

The momentum may switch but at least make sure it's because your opponent gained it, not because you lost it. When the momentum is totally for you, it is crucial that you do not allow yourself to get distracted. This often happens because players are lulled into a sense of false security when things are heavily in their favour. They are playing well, their opponent may be playing badly and it seems fine to relax and enjoy completing the win.

Be warned! A big gap, made up of your best tennis plus your opponent's worst tennis, can become an increasingly smaller gap once your opponent starts to play a bit better and you drop a few careless points here and there. Your opponent then starts to feel better and therefore plays better, while you get frustrated because you know you shouldn't have relaxed and start to play worse. The whole thing can start to escalate and feed off itself.

Even if you are 5–1 up in the first set and you have won five times as many games as your opponent, do not be fooled by the score – it may not mean you are five times better than your opponent!

Understand the scoring system (it isn't football)

If this was a football match and the score was 5–1, then the team in the lead would be easing off, attempting to keep free from injury, saving themselves for the next match, coasting and probably playing relaxed exhibition football.

But tennis is not like football, where there is a fixed time limit to the match and where a 5–1 lead means almost certain victory. There is no time limit in tennis, and there are potential dangers for the player in the lead because no one can be sure exactly where the finish line is!

Don't be fooled into thinking you've got a bigger lead than you have. A 5–1 lead suggests you've only got to win one of the next four games, and any one will do. Statistically true of course, but if you play a couple of loose games and your opponent gets encouraged and gains momentum 5–3 will feel very different, particularly if you've missed a set point or two.

Know how you got there

If you relax without knowing why you have the lead, you probably won't notice if anything changes. It's like getting the first answer right in your maths exam without knowing why, and being pleased with yourself none the less. You are likely to pay a price for your complacency.

Are you winning because you are controlling the tactics, or because you have been winning close games on one-off happenings against the run of play? For example, these might be net cords, bad calls by the umpire or the first two passing shots you hit this year! If the latter is true, then you should still be guarding against a flow change because these things are not completely controllable by you.

On the other hand, if you got to 4–1 up because your own tactics and superior play are working, you can relax a little (but not too much) because you understand why you are 4–1 ahead.

Be prepared to fight

You have to be prepared to fight to keep your lead. People who are losing tend to play better because they nearly always relax and play as if they have nothing to lose. They are also likely to change tactics as a last roll of the dice. Nothing focuses the mind like impending doom!

It may seem illogical, but at 5–1 up you must be alert to these possibilities and therefore be prepared to increase your own level of intensity and to work even harder. **Fighting spirit is not only needed when you are behind.** It is not comforting to know you may have to work harder when you've played some of your best tennis to reach this position, but it is the best way of ensuring that the momentum remains with you, particularly if you are close to winning the match. Players like Julia, in the example given at the beginning of the book, will not go down without a fight – so be prepared to fight and be surprised if you don't have to. It's always better that way round – **hope for the best, but prepare for the worst.**

Win the first point

Winning the first point of the game is important at any time, but it is sometimes neglected when you are in the lead. When players are losing they can lose hope quickly. The first point of each game, particularly when you are playing a tired opponent, can encourage or discourage them at a time when they may be clinging onto any last signs of hope before they lose heart.

Watch for a change in tactics

Knowing how you got there allows you to spot a change in the tactics of your opponent more quickly. You may not know the answer to your opponent's new tactics, but at least don't be caught out by realising they've changed only when they have drawn level.

If your opponent does change tactics be sure to renew your efforts. Players who are losing change tactics because they are desperate. Whatever they change to is going to be their second choice (because nobody would keep their first choice up their sleeve to change to in an emergency). Therefore they are unlikely to stick to their tactics for long if you renew your focus and combat them well.

Step up a gear

As long as you are aware of the above, now is the time you can gamble, take more risks and try to step up a gear.

You can use the cushion of a lead to try and kill off the match if it's getting near the end. Or if it's not near the end, you may step up and play so well that your opponent thinks you are invincible, which in turn may have a big effect on the outcome of the match. For this reason, some players make it a policy to step up every time they have created some daylight between them and their opponent.

Tactically, you can afford to gamble a little. As long as it is a calculated gamble and you are ready to return to your tactics as soon as you feel things slightly start to slip, then go for it: take the ball earlier, hit big returns off first serves, serve and volley if you like.

It's also a good time to vary your game. You are feeling good, so variations are more likely to work. In all likelihood, your opponent won't realise you vary only when the momentum is totally with you, they'll just remember that you may vary it.

However, players can slip up when doing this, when they keep gambling for too long and keep giving their opponent cheap points trying to hit winners, sometimes to make up for the ones they missed! Of course, cheap points are exactly what your opponent wants when they are well behind – *it's easier climbing steep hills with a helping hand up.*

Mentally, you can afford to step up as well. The best way to do this is to relax your mind and allow yourself the freedom of going for your shots. An international coach from Croatia once told me: 'Talent is inside you. It stays trapped inside when your mind and body are tense. It can only flow out when you are relaxed.'

During this relaxed state of focus it is possible to take your game to higher levels. Many tennis players and athletes have experienced it and it has become known as *being in the zone* or *playing out of your head.*

When your mind is clear, you are capable of very high levels of tennis. Just think about how many perfect returns you have hit after you called the serve out. To relax your mind and let things happen when the points are live takes practice and courage, but it can be done.

When the momentum is totally with you, it's a good time to begin learning about this type of stepping up a gear.

(Much has been written in sport about how to quieten your mind to achieve this state of *being in the zone*. If you are interested in learning more about this, I recommend *The Inner Game of Tennis*, Gallwey, WT 1986).

When momentum is totally with you

When momentum is with you
When momentum is neutral
When momentum is against you
When momentum is totally against you

Key points:

- Avoid the dangers.
- Understand the scoring system (it isn't football).
- Know how you got there.
- Fighting spirit is not only needed when behind.
- Win the first point.
- Watch for a change in tactics.
- Step up a gear.

When Momentum is With You

There are many similarities between this stage and the previous stage. However, potential turning points are more important when momentum is with you because you have less of a cushion to fall back on. In the previous stage, ie *when momentum is totally with you*, you have longer (though as we saw, not too long) to get your attitude right because your opponent has to make up a lot of ground.

Put the radar on

When momentum is with you, if you don't spot a potential turning point and react to it, things could turn against you. You therefore need to have your *turning points radar* switched on. Like my county captain, Mike Robinson once said: 'Winning from a winning position is like drowning someone. Every time their head pops up above the water, you push it back down again!'

Keeping the radar on is like keeping an eye for their heads popping back up!

Potential turning points were covered in *Chapter One*. But remember, they always relate to one of three things:

- *The actions of your opponent.*
- *Your own actions.*
- *External events that affect one or both of you (including the scoring system).*

They all have one thing in common: the potential to cause a change in the balance of the mental energy of one player or the other, which then causes a change in the momentum flow of the match.

When you spot a potential turning point, you need to be ready to raise your intensity and effort because potential turning points need not become actual turning points.

Turning point or blip?

At the end of the match, a potential turning point will either be a turning point against you, ie the moment when everything turns around and your opponent takes control, or it will be merely a blip – an awkward moment before the momentum continues to go with you.

The idea of potential turning points being also potential blips (depending on the player's reaction) occurred to me because of two experiences:

1   Watching unseeded players at Wimbledon some years ago, there were several examples of players having match points, missing the opportunity and then crashing to heavy defeat in the final set. Yet I would see the top players double-fault perhaps twice when serving for the match and still going on to win the tie-break. Why didn't they also crash to defeat in the final set?

2   Watching inexperienced and experienced players on clay, I noticed that if the inexperienced players missed an opportunity they seemed to panic. The clay-court specialists, on the other hand, accepted missing opportunities and didn't panic. They were prepared to stay on court for three hours if necessary and did not have a *crash* mentality.

How to control potential turning points against you

When potential turning points occur, it's as if the momentum suddenly and momentarily becomes neutral. If a player reacts negatively during that time, you can sense the momentum beginning to turn. Even non-tennis playing spectators can sense this feeling – they can relate to the human reaction of something going wrong and the implications of this. They sense it is the player's response immediately after a potential turning point that determines how big an effect it will have on the match.

Potential turning points are always things that can depress or boost you or your opponent. When you have the lead, they usually take the form of **distractions to you and/or positive changes by your opponent.**

John McEnroe is an example of a player who often benefited from this double change in energy. He brought about match flow changes through his arguments with the umpire. These incidents usually ended up with him feeling fired mentally with his opponent having gone cold physically and probably distracted mentally by the long interruption.

The real dynamite for changing momentum is when both distractions to you and positive changes to your opponent happen together and feed off each other. **It is your job never to let them happen together when you have the lead.**

Changeovers are a good opportunity to psych yourself up for raising your intensity

*Arguments with the umpire can affect the flow of the match –
it is your reaction to these arguments that really matters*

Key factors that will determine your ability to control potential turning points against you include:

- *attitude and fighting spirit*
- *body language*
- *collecting points*
- *dealing with gamesmanship*
- *choosing the battlefield*
- *keeping the match running*
- *choking – your attitude towards it.*

Attitude and fighting spirit

You may not be able to control your opponent's attitude, but you can control yours. If a turning point has just happened against you and your opponent suddenly raises their energy/game because they feel good, you have to be prepared to quickly raise your energy/game too, so your opponent doesn't get the momentum. It's like running a race and your opponent decides to kick – you have to respond. If you do this well, your opponent may lose heart if their best attempt to catch you up has failed.

This is how real fighting spirit is born. If you learn to react to disappointing events (ie potential turning points) with the untypical reaction of not letting them get you down, then you will at least be lessening the potential swing to your opponent.

Part of getting this attitude right happens before you go on court. Think for a minute about how many perfect matches you have played. Most of the players I know have played hundreds of matches but can only ever recall a few perfect matches. Of all the things we don't know about your next match, we can at least be sure of one thing – at some stage something will go wrong. Therefore, prepare your mind for something going wrong – make sure you are psyched up for any potential turning points against you so that you are ready to respond positively.

With the right attitude you can keep potential turning points against you in your favour. Saving break point is a good example of this. You may have had something go wrong to have break point against you, but if you win it and go on to win the game, it actually creates more momentum for you than just winning a game in a straightforward manner.

Tim Henman has a very good attitude to this. He recovers mentally very quickly after missing a shot to give his opponent break point. Many times he digs himself back out again with service winners or brilliant play. This can work in his favour, even if it doesn't do much for the nerves of his supporters!

Body language

Even if you can't control your energy, you need to at least control how it looks to your opponent. If they get a boost from what's happening in the match (eg a big winner, a double fault, an unexpected missed smash) you don't want to double this boost by letting them see you are downcast.

It is vital to remember that *a potential turning point will end up as a turning point or merely a blip depending on your response to what happens.* **It's not what goes wrong, but your response to what goes wrong that matters.** You have to be mentally prepared to renew your efforts if you slip up when in the lead. Remember that *fighting spirit is not only needed when you are behind.*

Collecting points

When momentum is with you, you should keep the play rolling. Try to collect as many points as possible. Statistics show that the player who wins the most points will win the match with very few exceptions. Momentum may well shift in time. During the time it is with you, stay focused and collect as many points as possible to add to your overall tally. Do not relax and think that you can afford to lose a few sloppy points because things are going your way.

As any farmer will tell you, make hay while the sun shines!

Dealing with Gamesmanship

Players who have the momentum against them and feel they are running out of time sometimes use gamesmanship. This is because players who are losing get more desperate. It is basically an attempt to cause a distraction so you lose your focus. It often works because you tend to relax a bit when things are going for you and can get distracted more easily.

Understanding what these players are trying to do can help you keep your focus. Gamesmanship is all about distraction; it usually involves, at best bending the rules, and at worst cheating. This can cause feelings of unfairness that can divert some of your mental energy from the game itself.

Players who resort to gamesmanship usually pretend to be ignorant of the problem they are causing while knowing there are no rules to deal with it effectively. This adds to the feeling of unfairness and increases your distraction.

Choosing the battlefield

Matches can be won or lost either on a tennis or non-tennis (ie gamesmanship) basis. It's like having two battlefields on which two different battles are fought. On one battlefield there is the tennis game; on the other is the gamesmanship game.

If your opponent can't win on the tennis battlefield, they might try to entice you onto the gamesmanship battlefield, particularly on a big point. Do not be tempted to go there. Winning battles is a lot to do with who gets to choose the battlefield. If your opponent is trying gamesmanship, they have probably found it to work before and have been practising on that battlefield for a long time. It is their home ground. Therefore, stay on your winning battlefield – the tennis battlefield.

In other words, if it's a questionable line call, don't get involved in arguing if you are in the lead and you know it will distract you. Make your point strongly and keep the match about tennis by refocusing on the game itself.

Negative body language can turn the flow of the match against you

Beware! There are many forms of gamesmanship including:

- **Toilet breaks**

  These can give your opponent time to recover and let you go off the boil, either by allowing time for you to be distracted mentally or by ensuring you go cold physically. Be sure to keep warm, use the time to review which tactics are working and be ready for your opponent to renew their efforts when they return.

- **Bad line calls**

  If you do not have an umpire, and you receive a bad line call, it is very easy to be distracted. Here is an example of how you can react positively to a bad line call:

  - Walk to the net and calmly but strongly ask your opponent if they are sure it was out.

  - If they say yes, ask how far out it was.

  - Say you thought it was in and ask if they are prepared to play the point again.

  - If they are not, continue with the game and put your focus into concentrating on the tennis. This is crucial because you do not want long interruptions when you have the momentum.

Be prepared to work hard.

If you do have an umpire you can also query the call but then continue soon after for the same reasons. Because of the time it takes, it is not worth getting the referee to come to the court when you have the momentum with you, because the end result is almost certainly that *the wind will go out of your sails.*

- **Biased clapping**

    When you make a mistake you naturally feel down. When your opponent's supporters clap your mistake they hope to make you feel worse, to the point of distracting you from the game. Remember this, and don't fall into the trap of glaring at them or appealing to their sense of fairness; you may as well pull faces at the sun when it shines in your eyes on a smash! Stay focused on the tennis.

Keeping the match running

When you have the momentum with you, don't create distractions against yourself. Keep the match running. When things are going your way, the quicker the match finishes the better, so don't slow it down. Some players, such as Andre Agassi, speed up and actually run between points when they have the flow with them – this gives their opponent less chance to refocus mentally.

Don't interrupt the match by arguing a line call too long, taking a toilet break or taking too long between points. Avoid interruptions when you have the momentum.

In one match, one of the players I coached was leading 6–2, 3–1 and 30–40 when he decided to retrieve a ball that had been hit three courts away, even though he had two balls with which to serve. His three-minute absence allowed his opponent to regroup and regain some momentum for himself by feeling as if it was the start of the match again. This player effectively created a turning point against himself and he eventually lost in three sets.

Make sure you are well prepared. Plan ahead before matches so that you cope with anything that might frustrate you, causing a distraction. Make sure you have with you anything you might need: spare rackets correctly strung, drinks, plasters, spare shoelaces, change of shirt etc.

Choking

A player choking is perhaps the best known way of a player creating a turning point against themselves. Because it is perceived to be a mentally weak thing to do, if a player loses a lead through choking, they can then be affected mentally for the rest of the match as well – it usually causes their self-esteem to plummet.

Players can choke for many different reasons and I am not going to try to cover them all here. There are many sports psychology explanations and different tools to deal with it, ranging from relaxation techniques to positive imagery.

However, if you are a tennis expert you should know how tough it can be on occasions to close out a win. It is only the non-experts who believe that losing a lead is a sign of weakness every time.

To keep choking in perspective, remember what a tennis expert knows:

- There's no point in getting very nervous. If your opponent is any good, they will be fighting harder and playing better at the end of the match, so you must always be prepared to work hard for another five minutes or more. How do you expect to win the last game? Will any opponent who is a good player tamely dump four balls into the bottom of the net for you? Concentrate on your own game rather than rely on errors from your opponent.

- Be prepared to work hard; nobody knows where the finish line might be. Even at match point, there is still work to be done. Be a tennis expert and be prepared to fight.

When momentum is totally with you
When momentum is with you
When momentum is neutral
When momentum is against you
When momentum is totally against you

Key points:

- Put the radar on to make sure potential turning points against you are merely blips.
- Fighting spirit is not only needed when you are behind.
- It's not what goes wrong that matters, it's your reaction to it.
- Accumulate points – it will have a wearing effect on opponents.
- Learn to deal with gamesmanship – choose the right battlefield.
- Keep the match running, especially when you're in the lead.
- Keep choking in perspective – be a tennis expert.

When Momentum is Neutral

Neutral momentum is when things are *in the balance* – when the scales are waiting to be tipped by one player or the other. It can be an unnerving or exciting feeling, because things could swing either way.

It exists when there is an equal match in the standards and often the energy levels of the two players. The most exciting and memorable times this happens is when both players are at their best and involved in an epic tussle. If this is set against a background of neutral momentum then the atmosphere is electric with hopes, fears and anticipation. This happened in The Davis Cup 1999 tie, GB versus the USA.

The match score stood at two rubbers all and in the final match, Greg Rusedski stood at two sets all with Jim Courier – as the set advanced still the deadlock remained. The crowd was at fever pitch, television audiences were soaring by the minute and the players became gladiators more than tennis players.

Courier and the USA went on to win, but as Peter Fleming, the TV commentator said, so did the sport of tennis. Neutral momentum is rarely as exciting as in tennis because the players don't have teammates to pass the ball to and no time limit will cut short the battle of wills.

However, at other times, neutral momentum can exist when it seems as if nothing much is happening, rather like two boxers sparring. At football matches, crowds go quiet when the momentum is neutral in this way and players are passing the ball around without any obvious attacking inclinations.

It can happen at the beginning of the match. It can also occur well into the match, when neither player can find their rhythm and the game is full of errors from both players (such as when neither player seems able to hold their serve).

Jim Courier – a player who refuses to give in during the heat of battle

For example, there can be neutral momentum when the match is 2–2 in the second set, even though one player is a set ahead, or when it is 5–4 in the final set, which makes for the most exciting tennis.

Whenever it occurs though, it is the time when chances for surging ahead need to be created and taken.

Don't wait

When the momentum is neutral, you need to be ready to grab it. The player who waits in this situation is like a sprinter waiting on the line for their rival to shout 'go'. At this point you should be looking to establish a flow of momentum in your favour.

If you wait for your opponent to do something, it is possible that you will end up following the flow of momentum and raising your game too late to win the set. In days gone by, it was more possible to wait, in the hope your opponent would act first and make a mistake. These days, the saying *he who hesitates is lost* is more appropriate.

You often hear of players nearly pulling off such an upset, then consoling themselves with the thought that there was nothing they could do when it came to it, because their opponent came up with the goods. Usually this is because they waited for something to happen.

Grab it

When the momentum is neutral, higher-ranked players will often raise their game, spurred on by the realisation that they must act before it's too late. But how should you grab it? What do you do to raise your game? In what way should you act?

It can be tactically. It could be to zone in on specific tactics you have discussed with your coach before the match. Sometimes, if your opponent is looking nervous, grabbing the momentum may mean showing them you are *up for the fight* and making them play every ball by playing percentage tennis.

On the other hand, there may be times when percentage tennis is not enough. Recently I was captain (on-court) for Britain when we played Spain in the semi-final of the European Championship. We lost in the final set of the final doubles. We had played high levels of tennis that would have beaten most teams, but the fact is we didn't find the levels of exceptional tennis that the Spanish found when the momentum was neutral. We were devastated. Sometimes you need more than percentage tennis.

Whatever you do, decide quickly and do it. *Keep the future in your hands.*

Be ready before you begin

To grasp the opportunity to surge ahead in the match can often mean being properly psyched up to do so before the match begins.

This is particularly true if you are playing an opponent you are not expected to beat. You have to be mentally ready to *stick the knife in* if the opportunity of neutral momentum comes along. Don't wait to see what happens, because the opportunity will disappear quickly against the better players. (If you don't like the idea of *sticking the knife in* you can always *grasp the nettle, push them over the cliff* or *take the bull by the horns!*)

> A phrase used by Tim Henman's coach, David Felgate, before playing matches against higher ranked players, was *step up to the plate* (a baseball phrase). This came about after Tim lost a number of matches to better players early in his career and seemed happy to have played well. David felt he may have looked good but was never really in the match as a serious contender when key moments came up.

Come back and go

Grabbing the situation might simply mean urging yourself to forge ahead to win when you have pulled back from being well behind. Very often you will see a player come back and draw level, only to relax and lose the set.

There are many examples of players who made a change in their game or renewed their efforts when they were behind, but as soon as they pulled level in the score, they thought the job was done and relaxed their fighting spirit. Their energy dropped. At the same time the player in the lead might have been fearing their opponent drawing level and when it happened they relaxed because their fears were realised. Sometimes this releases tension, sometimes it makes them angry. Either way their energy and fighting spirit often goes up.

This change in energy on court from either one or both players is why the momentum can switch again, and the player who has come back can lose. So, if you are the player who fights to draw level, be determined to keep fighting and surge ahead. Be aware that the game when the scores are level is key if you intend to win. Never draw level and wait to see what happens – **come back and go!**

Tim Henman knows he has to 'step up to the plate' to beat the better players

When momentum is totally with you
When momentum is with you
When momentum is neutral
When momentum is against you
When momentum is totally against you

Key points:

- Don't wait.
- Grab it.
- Be ready before you begin.
- Come back and go!

32

When Momentum is Against You

When the flow of the match is against you, it can be frustrating. This is particularly true if things are against you because you haven't played that well.

Your opponent may seem to be playing with increased energy and confidence and key points seem to go against you. Things that normally work, or maybe were working earlier on in the match, now just keep narrowly failing. If luck plays its part, it doesn't seem to be in your favour. Small things that don't irritate you when you have the momentum with you, are now distractions. It can feel as if you are swimming against the tide.

However, you are not alone, all players experience these feelings. The feeling is captured in a couple of verses of a little known poem:

> *You bob and weave and duck and dive,*
> *Yet he just seems to flow,*
> *With lots of time to choose his shots,*
> *While you're a yard too slow.*
>
> *So you madly sprint across the court,*
> *In a frenzied show of power,*
> *While the ball just floats the other way,*
> *At fourteen miles an hour!*

Alistair Higham, *Off the Frame*

At such moments it is easy to feel that things are slipping away and to become frustrated. Your body language may begin to tell the story of your feelings and give even more encouragement to your opponent. How best do you deal with this situation? Without doubt, you could be on a slippery slope if you're not careful.

Show fighting spirit

It is when things are against you that you need to show fighting spirit. Who caused the problems doesn't matter. It might be you, your opponent or the umpire. The only important thing is that you have problems and you need to have the right spirit to solve them.

Sometimes, fighting spirit is simply a question of being doggedly determined not to be put off. A bit like a terrier who refuses to let go of a stick.

Sometimes, you need to see things differently – to see the positive side. Of course problems are really challenges. The trick is to learn to see them as challenges. As Einstein once said, 'In the middle of difficulty, lies opportunity'.

For example, in an international match against the Czech Republic recently, I was sitting on the court with the British number one junior, Anne. Every little thing that could go wrong was going wrong. Line calls went against her, net cords went against her, and on top of everything else, she had had match points in the second set but lost it. She was now a break down in the third set.

Indeed so many things had gone wrong that it occurred to me that if I sat down off court and tried to design a tougher test of tennis character with a paper and pen, I probably couldn't. At the next changeover I told her I couldn't design a tougher test than this, so if she wanted a reputation of being mentally tough then she had to pass this test.

This view of things helped her see the challenge as a positive one. Her on court energy became more positive, she raised her game and showed great fighting spirit. Not only did the momentum swing her way, but also she kept it. She saw everything that went wrong as an opportunity to prove herself and came through to win the match.

Most players get frustrated when the flow of the match is against them – how do you deal with it?

Don't rush

Earlier I said that if the momentum is with you, the quicker the match finishes the better. It follows that when the momentum is against you, the longer you are on court the better. So it is vital you take your time between points and don't allow yourself to be rushed.

This is sometimes not so easy to do. The natural reaction to having things go against you is to want to make them right quickly. However, rushing when you have things go against you and you are feeling in turmoil inside can only lead to more errors. The same one-off quick wonder winners that hit the line when things go for you are the ones that miss the line when you're up against it.

Keep a check on your body language

In wars, planes fly over the enemy dropping leaflets telling them bad news, for example their supplies are running out, their superiors have not told them that many of their soldiers have surrendered, and they should give up now before they are killed. Tennis is not war, but certainly you should not be letting your opponent know when you're not feeling as good as you would like!

Keep a look out for your opponent's body language – you may be able to sense a potential turning point

Switch on the radar

You need to keep on *a constant lookout for potential turning points*. Even though the natural reaction may be to think that the fates are against you, you need to keep a radar for turning points firmly switched on.

A player I coach was once losing an international match. She was 0–4 and the momentum was against her, but only just. The match was very close, with each game tightly contested and my player losing only because her opponent was hitting a few one-off winners. But, crucially, my player was reading the score rather than the match and as a consequence was feeling quite demoralised.

Perhaps because she was feeling low, she failed to seize two opportunities that were created for turning the momentum her way. One was a drop-dead net cord winner at game point down; the other a brilliant passing shot played by her from an almost impossible position.

While not registering the significance of the points she won, my player had managed none the less to get herself back to 2–4 down when another golden opportunity presented itself. She again failed to spot it. A man came onto the courts with the purpose of watering them, not realising that a junior international match was being played.

My player could have used this distraction to her advantage by realising the potential opportunity for her opponent to become anxious about her lead being eroded. Yet my player became more irritated and upset by the disruption than her opponent and lost an opportunity to bring about a swing in momentum in her favour.

You should welcome outside distractions, the more the better ... for **your opponent** to be distracted.

Keep an eye on your opponent

Watch the body language of your opponent and remember to keep doing it. If you were a boxer, this would be easy, because you are only a few feet away; in tennis you have to look closely and regularly if you want to pick up any signals.

Many turning points will occur in the mind of your opponent. Who knows, they may be carrying an injury, may be worried that they will lose a lead because they regularly do or may not be happy with the tension of a new racket.

You may not know what causes turning points, but you may be able to sense them if you keep an eye on how your opponent is feeling. The key is to watch them regularly and not just after really obvious potential turning points.

How to control potential turning points for you

When a potential turning point happens in your favour, you should allow it to give you a boost and show this in your body language. Your opponent might not have recognised it as a potential turning point and extra energy from you might introduce a doubt into their mind.

You will often see an experienced player visibly pick up in their energy when this happens. They will be livelier in their routine before the point starts, they may call out the score with more confidence in their voice and may shout 'Come on' to themselves.

Players who have had momentum turn suddenly against them before, may start to worry when they see your reaction. Again, don't forget that the bigger the swing in mental energy at times like this, the bigger the swing in momentum.

Two things to help you control potential turning points are:

- *learning to spot them quicker by having a positive attitude*
- *maintaining a lead by using your imagination.*

Spot potential turning points quickly by having a positive attitude

Having your potential turning points radar switched on is important but it is your speed of thought in recognising them and renewing your efforts that is key. Your general attitude can help this process considerably. If you always see the bright side of a situation it can make a big difference. For example you can either see the glass as half empty or half full. Learn to see it as half full.

Here are two examples of how such an attitude can help renew efforts quickly and gain momentum.

- One day my mother, who is a low-level club player, was playing a singles match in a tournament in Cumbria. She had just lost the first set 7–6. I passed the back of the court and asked her how she was getting on. Her reply was revealing. 'Oh really well,' she said. I wished her luck and left the match, wondering if her comment was meant to be sarcastic.

  She went on to win the match and later I asked what she had meant by her comment. She replied, 'Well I was really pleased to get 6–7. At my level I lose so many matches heavily that I was quite encouraged to have lost the first set so closely. I was thinking to myself that if I could just change one or two things I had a good chance of levelling the match.'

Such an attitude is a very positive one, but it is rare, because the emotion involved in going one set down when you might have been one set up can cloud your view. Indeed, the score line 7–6, 6–0 is often seen because a close gap in mental energy can become a large gap if both players change, ie if one player is boosted by winning a close first set and the other is deflated.

- In a recent National Indoor Circuit match between two players, Alan and Jim, the first set went fairly comfortably to Alan, who was the higher-ranked player and expected to win. The second set was very closely contested and Jim just won it in a long drawn-out tie-break during which time he played well above himself. Jim sat down at the end of the second set – he was visibly relieved and excited. He relaxed, thinking the climax would come at the end of the third set, as it had done in the second, a bit like a story coming together at the end.

  However, there was to be no climax. At the beginning of the third set Alan changed his strategy, increasing his intensity and energy to win key points in the flow of the first three games. Before Jim could raise his intensity levels to an equivalent degree, he was 0–3 and the match had effectively slipped from his grasp. Alan had been able to renew his efforts after a disappointing second set because he stayed positive and was much better tuned in to the opportunities presented by the beginning of a new set.

> Having a positive attitude allows you to see possibilities in situations that a negative attitude prevents you from seeing. It allows the outlook to be bright rather than dull. Former Wimbledon champion, Jimmy Connors, once said he never lost a tennis match, he just occasionally ran out of time before he found out how to win!

Maintain a lead by using your imagination

Sometimes momentum can be going against you when you are in the lead. Again, your attitude to events can make a big difference in how things end up.

Whatever the situation, it's rarely as bad as it seems when you take the emotion out of it. Imagine you are 6–4, 5–1 and your opponent comes back to 5–4. With only two minutes at the changeover you may not get your mental approach right to renew your energy.

But imagine you were able to travel back in time to before the match began and someone offered you 6–4, 5–4 as a score line to start the match with, instead of 0–0, and gave you two hours to get ready. You would surely arrive ready to play and psyched up. Well, we haven't discovered time travel yet, but you can get the same attitude simply by learning to renew your efforts more quickly.

How to create turning points in your favour

As well as keeping the radar on to spot potential turning points, you should try to create turning points. There are many ways you can help create turning points in your favour through your own actions:

- *Changing tactics*
- *Not changing tactics*
- *Winning the best rallies*
- *Spotting patterns of play*

Changing tactics

You could consider changing tactics. *Chapter Three* looks at the whole area of tactics in detail, but for now here is an example of how changing tactics can turn a match around.

- In my younger days, I played for a German Club in the Bavarian leagues. Having been flown over by the club and being paid by the club for playing as their number one player, I was keen to make a good impression.

On the first day I asked about my opponent's style and was told in a thick German accent: 'He can rally for 100 shots, is very fit and never misses a passing shot'. Being more used to grass than clay, this was not what I wanted to hear. I decided to go for quick winners as rallying was obviously pointless. I lost 6–0, 6–2 in less than an hour.

Fortunately I won the doubles to win the tie that day, but was not looking forward to the singles match next day. It came all too soon and in the morning I enquired about my next opponent. The reply came again, but this time seemed to be delivered in an even heavier tone: 'He can rally for 100 shots, is very fit, never misses a passing shot ... and is ranked four places above the player you lost to yesterday'. 'Hhhmmm' I thought.

The match started, and with no real plan things started to go against me from the start. I felt downhearted. Then at one changeover I decided, more out of interest than anything else, to see if he could rally for a hundred shots. I began to count the shots in each rally and literally did nothing else for the rest of the match. The longest rally we had was 26 shots and I won 6–4, 6–1. Nobody was more surprised than me!

Not changing tactics

Sometimes you may not need to change tactics, but simply do what you are doing better, or allow it time to have its effect.

You may be dominating the points every time you get your first serve in but missing too many first serves. You may also have worked very good openings and come to the net only to miss a couple of crucial smashes, which has tilted things against you. The answer in this case would be to continue but to get more first serves in and not to miss the smashes after working for the opening.

On the other hand, if you are playing good consistent tennis, but have lost a close first set, you may not need to change. Consistent baseline play that maintains a level sometimes takes time to have its effect on the opponent. The effect is like that of an arm wrestle. If you keep the pressure on for long enough then the opponent will wilt. Some sooner, some later, depending on their mental toughness.

Winning the best rallies

There are times in a match when both players play their best tennis at the same time, in quality rallies. This may happen in only one or two rallies or it may happen in several, sometimes close together. If you can win these rallies, it can create a turning point in your favour. This is because of the mental effect on a player of losing the point despite playing their best tennis. Seeing their best shots returned with interest is depressing! If this happens a few times, a player may just accept that you are the better player and begin to lose hope of winning. How many times? Well, again, it depends on their mental toughness.

Spotting patterns of play

Knowing the likely patterns of your opponent can help create a turning point in your favour. You can scout your opponent to note their favourite patterns or you can simply observe carefully and gather information as the match goes on.

For example, a player may always smash to the backhand, or always kill into the gap, or always pass cross-court. If you make a mental note of these patterns, it allows you to make a best guess at a crucial time later in the match. If you snatch the type of point that your opponent had been winning (eg you lobbing, them smashing) on a big point, this could create a turning point in your favour.

Fair play

Never attempt to create turning points by bending the rules. The enjoyment of winning is very closely linked to the enjoyment of overcoming the obstacles during the journey towards winning. Don't let that journey be tainted by use of gamesmanship. Keep your tennis on the tennis battlefield.

When momentum is totally with you
When momentum is with you
When momentum is neutral
When momentum is against you
When momentum is totally against you

Key points:

- Show fighting spirit.
- Don't rush.
- Keep a check on your body language.
- Switch on the radar.
- Keep an eye on your opponent.
- Spot potential turning points quickly by having a positive attitude.
- Maintain a lead by using your imagination.
- Review your tactics.
- Win the best rallies.
- Spot patterns of play.
- Never use gamesmanship.

When Momentum is Totally against You

When the momentum is totally against you, it is the easiest thing in the world to believe it's just not your day. If you are, for example, 4–1 down in the third set, having been a set up, it can seem that it's too big a hill to climb to turn things around and that the flow of the match is irreversibly with your opponent. It's at times like these that you can wonder why you bother playing at all. It is also easy to display negative body language, thus giving your opponent even more encouragement.

The fact is, however, that matches do turn around regularly from seemingly impossible positions. You are only in a *stage of momentum,* and if you can get out of it to the next level then turning points become more possible and the nerves of your opponent may work in your favour. If you are to make a comeback, this bit is the most difficult. Moving up a stage when you are well behind is mentally tougher than moving up a stage at any other time.

Don't lose hope

The most important thing when the momentum is totally against you, is not to lose hope. It is difficult, because your opponent is full of confidence, has the cushion of a lead and is trying to finish you off. That would be tough enough at any time, but it usually happens when you are probably feeling frustrated, disheartened and maybe tired having spent some time and energy getting yourself into this unfavourable position!

Your opponent may seem to be playing too well for you to have a chance of victory, but you should remember how easy it is to play well when the momentum is totally with you. It is the same for them. They won't be as good when the momentum has shifted.

The road to making a comeback is steep at first but it will get easier if you can dig in and get a foothold. Once you have got stuck in and begun to make a comeback, two factors will work in your favour: you will begin to feel better and your opponent will dislike the fact that it's not as easy as it was. This double change in energy gives the best conditions for a change in the flow of the match.

Take your time and play one point at a time

When the momentum is totally against you, take your time. Let the steam go out of your opponent's game. You have to take the time allowed and find some way of getting points on the scoreboard. Momentum in this situation tends to change slowly, (the creeping change mentioned earlier), and you have to build the foundations for a change.

Playing one point at a time is very important. When you are well behind in momentum, it is not possible just to collect points quickly like you can when you are in the lead. It's a bit like trying to get out of a pit. Put great emphasis on every step.

One game can make all the difference. If you can stay in touch with your opponent on the scoreboard when you are well behind in momentum, you will be closer for when things turn around. For example, if you can somehow hold onto your serve when you are 1–4 in the final set, then 2–4 is a lot closer than 1–5 if your opponent starts to wobble or you start to build some momentum.

This is where the phrase *weathering the storm* applies. You hear it in other sports as well. In football, in this situation, getting the ball and somehow keeping

Don't lose hope – keep battling when things are against you

possession of it is crucial. The same applies in tennis – you have to find a way of staying in the match. Staying in the match is the best way of building foundations for a change in the future (eg a potential turning point that occurs when you are not so far behind in the momentum).

It is particularly important not to lose hope when you are tired. You never know how tired your opponent is as well. Don't let things slide. Stay in touch with the score by trying to win the first point of each game and taking each point one at a time.

Have a cunning plan

Here's an interesting ploy: if you are one set up, but well behind in the second set of a three-set match, you might consider the effect of starting the final set fresh, having had a few games in which you can, as it were, take a break from the tactics and intensity of play which won you the first set.

You can actually take advantage of being well behind in the second set by deliberately playing *exhibition tennis*, as if to create the impression that you are no longer trying or no longer care about the outcome of the match. The plan is twofold and in a sense is a win-win ploy.

If you lose the second set, you lull your opponent into a sense of false security so that for the crucial start of the third set you can hit your opponent with different tactics and/or a new attitude. However, you may not lose the second set. This approach of exhibition tennis may allow you to unsettle your opponent with quick, spectacular *one-off* wins to get yourself quickly out of *the momentum totally against you* stage. It is then possible to revert to the strategy that won you the first set knowing: that you have got back the necessary momentum, and that your opponent's nerves may become a factor as you continue with your comeback.

Read the future

Momentum moves through the five stages outlined above, and sometimes you cannot control it. Therefore be wise, realise there is a strong chance that it may change. Let that knowledge give you hope when you are well behind and keep you alert to dangers when you are well in front.

The key is to control your own mental energy (see *Controlling your energy* on page 57) and watch for signs of your opponent's change in mental energy, particularly after obviously significant events.

Remember what makes momentum turn:

* *A change in your opponent's mental energy – either gradual or sudden.*

* *A change in your mental energy – either gradual or sudden.*

When momentum is totally with you.
When momentum is with you.
When momentum is neutral.
When momentum is against you.

When momentum is totally against you.

Key points:

- Don't lose hope.
- Take your time and play one point at a time.
- Have a cunning plan.
- Read the future.

The Underlying Current of Momentum

As I said earlier, knowing the above is like having a compass and a map which you can apply to the journey of any match and any situation, no matter how different they are.

However, there is one thing that obviously can tilt the balance in favour of one player. It is relative standards. In other words, if one player simply has a higher standard, the underlying current of momentum will be in their favour and no matter what the lesser player does, they will always be more in danger of things going against them.

For example, let's look at Henman versus Sampras. Currently, Sampras at his best will beat Henman at his best. In other words, Sampras' 10/10 is better than Henman's 10/10.

Therefore, in order for Henman to have a chance of winning, he needs to play at 10/10 and needs Sampras to play at 7/10. If the match gets close and Sampras wins a big point and his energy goes up and Henman's goes down, the momentum can slide massively in favour of Sampras because of the distance between Sampras at 10/10 and Henman at 8/10.

Neutral momentum suits the better player for this reason; they have more room to raise their game. This is why the lesser player must grab the opportunity when it arises.

However, the fact that players don't always play their best tennis all the time explains why no match is without opportunities for the worse player and conversely, why no match is totally plain sailing for the better player. Matches do not go, for example 1–0, 2–0, 3–0 in a uniform way for the better player. In other words, at some stage in the match the better player may play under par and the worse player may play above par. If the worse player is watching for potential turning points, then they will always have a better chance of pulling off a shock win.

In tennis, as in all games, opportunities arise for both players, even if one player is of a higher standard. The unexpected will only happen, however, if the lesser player keeps taking chances and the better player fails to do the same.

Momentum and current form

How quickly momentum can switch is also affected by the current form of your opponent.

Lesser players enjoying a good run of form are obviously going to renew their efforts quicker and keep renewing them because their confidence is generally high. This is because confidence is linked closely to belief in being able to do a task. Players on form with some good recent results have greater belief than normal. This keeps their mental energy high for longer as recent experiences tell them it's worth it.

Similarly, players who are having a poor run of form, often find momentum swings against them more quickly. This is because they lose heart quicker which prevents them from renewing their efforts as quickly or for as long, as recent experiences tell them it's not worth it.

Here is an example of this:

- In a recent international match, a player lost 7–6, 1–6, 2–6. This player was rusty due to injury and so was nervous of her lack of any recent form. She was all right as long as things went for her. When they went against her she lost belief quickly as the score suggests.

  As form can significantly affect momentum in the match, choosing your tournaments to suit your form is important. Play down a level or two if you lack form and confidence in order to regain it. Play up a level or two if you have greater confidence.

Momentum and personalities

Another factor that can affect how momentum moves in a match is the personality of your opponent.

Most players are strongest in one stage of momentum and more vulnerable in others. For example, some players look invincible when they have the flow with them, but sometimes you may only have to get a small lead for their attitude, and consequently their play, to deteriorate.

Some reactive players are terrific when they are behind, showing real tenacious fighting qualities, but then seem to lose these qualities when they get in front. They don't seem to be comfortable being the one who is out in the lead. They prefer to battle from behind.

Some characters in tennis are fatalistic and tend to see turning points as marking the beginning of a disaster. Their heads can go down very quickly once the flow goes against them, with a feeling of *this always happens to me*. Such players often do not understand momentum, they have a superstitious view of it and think it normally only turns dramatically. For this reason they are as capable of dramatic comebacks as dramatic losses in momentum.

Some players seem to play terribly until the momentum is neutral and they just find the right shot at the right time. These types of players often nearly lose to players they shouldn't, but always just seem to pull through.

Other players are very moody and can change their energy in a flash. This sudden change in energy is common with South American and Italian temperaments. These Latin characters can create turning points simply because of their ability to change energy and focus quickly – they can be missing everything and feeling sorry for themselves one minute, and then the next minute be *on fire*. These players who have the ability to forget what's gone and quickly step up their energy can sometimes take best advantage of the scoring system. This is why moody players often turn matches around and are more successful than logic suggests they should be.

Then there are players who are simply inconsistent and play patchy tennis seemingly without any rhyme or reason. They may play flashy *one-off* shots – spectacular winners mixed with spectacular losers in any stage of momentum.

Use this knowledge to be prepared

If you know the character of your opponent and can recognise in which stage they are more effective, you are more likely to be able to anticipate the tough points and be ready accordingly.

For example, if your opponent is poor at closing out leads when things are going their way, then be prepared to take a lot of good play from them early on. You may not get a proper chance to win until you fight back from behind so keep competing hard. If they start to wobble, make them play a lot of balls so they have to earn their points.

If your opponent is known for starting slowly and always battling hard when behind, then be ready. Be prepared to raise your game and don't expect things to be easy just because you have the lead.

In some matches you might be up against a *flashy/patchy* player, who is capable of hitting superb *one-off* winners – **be ready for them**. Accept the fact that it might happen and don't panic when it does. Recognise that it can be unsettling to play these players because you may not feel in control due to the number of spectacular shots they can play. As you are likely to get some *cheap* points as well, don't rely on them, try to win some of the points in which they play spectacular shots.

In other matches, you may be playing a moody player. It is important not to provoke this type of player when they are feeling down and inward-looking. Let them dwell on their own problems while you stack up the points. A badly timed and intimidating 'Come on' against these players could turn their attention to the battle and away from how badly they are playing. This could be dangerous.

Think about the players you play against or know. When do they play best? What can you do to defeat them when they are in their favourite stage?

Look at your own game

The best players are those who are equally tough in all the stages of momentum. Think of the members of the England football team and who prefers which stage. The players who are good in them all are those that are worth the most money.

What would it take to turn yourself into a player who is excellent in any of the five situations? Which of the five situations are you weak in and why?

The possibilities for a player being poor in a given stage are endless so I will avoid giving too many examples. But be honest with yourself and identify areas for improvement. Then ask your coach to help or maybe even a sports psychologist. They have a whole array of mental tools for improving certain areas – from correct performance goal setting, to in between point routines, imagery, relaxation techniques and focus control. There are plenty of techniques (most of which are easy to understand and use) that can help you to improve your own individual momentum on court. Here are some examples:

- We have heard how Tim Henman's coach helped him to be good at *stepping up to the plate* when the momentum was neutral.

- Brad Gilbert, in his book *Winning Ugly*, (Gilbert, B and Jamison, S 1994) says his coach spotted that he used to be poor when he was ahead but very good when he was behind, so he used to kid himself he was losing whenever he was winning!

- Jim Courier, after he beat Greg Rusedski in the epic 1999 Davis Cup match against Great Britain, said he dealt with the huge crowd support for Rusedski by imagining he was in a rowing boat in a storm with waves crashing over, but it was his job to simply keep rowing.

- Martina Navratilova in her book *Tennis my Way* (Navratilova, M and Carillo, M 1983) said there were times when she relaxed too much after gaining a large lead over her opponent and said to herself 'It's in the bag'. She'd lose concentration, even feeling sorry for her *soon-to-be-vanquished* foe. She worked on correcting this by improving her concentration with specific exercises so that no uninvited thoughts disturbed her.

Key points:

- Current form and different personality traits can both affect momentum.
- Use this knowledge to anticipate and prepare for the tough points.
- Find your own solutions to keeping tough at crucial moments.

Chapter Three

Further Tips for Controlling Momentum

Potential Turning Points and the Score

Here is some good news. Although I have been
urging you to renew your efforts quickly and to play
the right tactics at the right moment, the truth is the
scoring system will let you get away with not getting
it right for quite some time and still allow you to
win. It's not advisable, but it is possible.

> Evonne Cawley (née Goolagong), who was
> Wimbledon Champion in 1980 sometimes used to
> disappear mentally for whole periods of the
> match. Evonne was from Australia and had
> aboriginal blood in her. Apparently the aborigines
> do wander off on their own for days at a time into
> the outback and this is known as *going
> walkabout.* Evonne would wander off mentally in
> matches so often that they used to say she'd
> *gone walkabout.* Yet she'd often still win.

So how is it that the scoring system lets you get
away with this?

The scoring system

In every match the scoring system gift-wraps ideal
opportunities for turning points to the player who is
losing. It happens because we have a unique,
frustrating, illogical, marvellous scoring system. The
scoring system is what makes tennis such an
unpredictable game, one in which the match is
never finished until it's finished.

It is a scoring system that makes for great excitement because it is not time-restricted; a tennis match does not finish because the players have been playing for 90 minutes. Nobody can ever be sure quite where the finishing line is going to be. The truth is that the scoring system favours the player who is behind. I was once on court with a player in an international match and, after 90 minutes, she was losing 6–1 3–0. She was nervous, distracted, erratic, showed poor body language, won only one game in the first ten and yet somehow went on to win the match.

Implications

Firstly, if you are behind, **never give up**, no matter how badly you are playing. The scoring system can effectively be a *get out of jail* card. However, if you are losing, you may only get one or two chances. This means your attitude is key. Poor play in a match can be forgotten as long as you **keep a positive attitude**.

So if you are the type of player who can't always guarantee being consistent (nearly all of us!) this is great news. Control what you can guarantee controlling – your attitude – and things could swing your way. Time your periods of maximum focus with these periods and you'll always be able to create opportunities for yourself.

Also, when you are in the lead, be aware that tennis will give your opponent a chance they may well not deserve. Be ready to renew your efforts at these times. Do not let them take you by surprise and when they come along, respect the scoring system and be prepared to tackle its *stings in the tail*. With this positive attitude, these moments, like all potential turning points, can be well negotiated as you continue forward.

Let's look at **when** these gift-wrapped opportunities occur.

Predicting potential turning points

While most potential turning points are unpredictable, those related to the score can be predicted easily. Knowing when the score will throw up turning points helps make you a better competitor. It gives you key landmarks for any tennis match.

Tennis coaches often refer to *big points* – the idea being that some points are worth more than others. These points give the best chance of turning the momentum in your favour. They are the times when only a few actual points played (or maybe even one point) have the best chance of impacting on a player's energy and thus changing the momentum. It is at these moments when a player has most to gain or lose.

A better term for these moments would be ***crucial times***. They commonly occur:

- *at the start of a set or*

- *at the end of a set – match point down.*

Starting a set

A new set is a new start. When a set is won or lost, it is easy to believe that the next set is bound to go the same way. In fact, the beginning of the next set gives you a great chance of a turning point. This is true of every start of a set but let's look at them individually:

- **Starting the first set**

  The beginning of the match is when the tone of the match is set. Early on the momentum is usually neutral. It is the first opportunity to establish the flow of the match in your favour. Get off on the wrong foot and you will have to make a change, so aim to get off on the right foot. This is done best by establishing your intentions, both tactical and mental, early on.

  If you intend to attack in the match then hit the second serve return hard right from the beginning. If you intend being the bigger personality in the match then show that right from the start with lots of positive energy. Whatever you intend, don't be slow coming out of the traps; momentum doesn't come your way if you wait for things to get going.

- **Starting the second set**

  Let's look at two extreme examples. Everything else falls in between the two extremes:

  ### *When the first set was 7–6*

  If you lose a very closely fought first set on a tie-break, and the momentum has gone against you, you can feel deflated as a result of *failing* when you were so close to establishing a lead. The second set can then very rapidly disappear before you have taken stock of the situation. By the same token, if you have just won a first set tie-break, if you can maintain the momentum and establish a 3–0 lead in the match, you will often be well on your way to winning.

  In both cases you need to refocus and renew your mental efforts very quickly, but it is more urgent if you have lost the set. The score-line 7–6 6–0 is often seen, as mentioned in Chapter 2, as a result of the swing in momentum at the beginning of the second set. This is because a close gap in mental energy can become a large gap if both players change (ie one's energy/confidence goes up and the other's goes down).

In both situations, during your two-minute break at the end of the first set, you should review the set and decide the best tactic to focus on at the crucial start of the next set. You may or may not need to change tactics. With 7–6, it may be a question of only changing small things.

When the first set was 6–0

The score 0–6, 0–0 represents a great opportunity for a turning point for the player who has the momentum against them. Having lost the first set 0–6 you may feel down mentally, but if you can win the next game your mental energy will go up dramatically. The player who was winning 6–0, but then trails at 0–1 may get frustrated by even such a minor change, and if it goes to 0–2, the match can be turned around by a big swing in momentum.

If you won the first set 6–0, you need to be aware of the dangers of 0–0. Don't be daunted by it, it's how the scoring system works. The best approach is to treat a new set as a new start. Forget the last one, even though you won it easily, and start again. You need to start again in your mind, because there is a difference from the last few games you played. During the last few games from 4–0 to 6–0, you had a big cushion and probably tried for more one-off shots. At 0–0, although you won the first set, you do not have the luxury of a lead of a few games. If things should swing against you briefly because your opponent has raised their game, then don't panic, hold your level and energy. Things are likely to swing back your way.

Whether you have won it or lost it, during your two-minute break at the end of the set, you should review the set and decide what is the best tactic to focus on at the crucial start of the second set. You may need to change tactics or you may need to be more consistent with the ones you have.

- **Starting the third set**

The start of the third set is another good chance for a turning point. If you have won the first set, but lost the second, you need to have a good start to the third to re-establish the momentum in your favour. It may be the first chance you have had to get a lead in the score for perhaps thirty minutes. If you win the first game, the fact you hold the lead has an effect on the mental energy of both you and your opponent. Let it be seen in your body language that you are renewing your efforts and are psyched up for the third set.

If you have won the second set, you need to put it out of your mind and quickly refocus. Give your opponent the impression that things will continue in the same pattern as the second set. Particularly if you win a tight second set where all the action was at the end, you might be fooled into relaxing, thinking that all the action will come at the end of the set. Of course it may, but whoever refocuses quickest may win the set because they won the first few games. Be prepared for your opponent to start again and renew their efforts – they will if they are any good.

NB Most of these principles that apply to the start of the third set also apply to the start of the second set.

You also need to be aware tactically. After two sets, you should have a lot of information about which tactics work best. As with the examples above, during your two-minute break at the end of the set, you should review the set and decide the best tactic to focus on at the start of the third set.

The beginning of any new set is a key potential turning point, a time at which there can be momentum shifts, and so it is vital to concentrate hard. Put the last set to one side in your mind and treat the new set as a new start.

A good start is important in all sports

Match point down

You can be 2–6 4–5 15–40, never having held the lead at any point during an hour and thirty-five minutes of play, and yet if you save the match points and win the set, you could be only five minutes from being equal in sets with the momentum with you. You always need to bear in mind that this scoring system favours the person who is losing. In football, the team in the lead could pack its defence and wait for the whistle ... but this is never true in tennis. Match point down may represent the best opportunity you've had in the match so far. Of course, a similar situation along with a similar swing in momentum can arise at set point down too.

Here are two examples of players who have turned a match around from being match point down:

- Becker v Nystrom – the year he went on to win Wimbledon the first time in 1985, Becker survived a match point against him in one of his earlier rounds.

- Andre Agassi beat Tim Henman in the 2000 Ericsson Open, after saving four match points. Henman, although he gave credit to Agassi for the way he played these crucial points was quoted: 'I won more points but at the end of the day I didn't win the important ones' (*Daily Mail*, 31 March 2000).

Combination effect

If, at a crucial time in a match, such as match point, something happens that at any other time would also class as a potential turning point (eg your opponent breaks a string), then this can create a bigger swing in momentum.

It can have a combination effect on a player. They feel down because they have lost the match point ... and their equipment is now broken! It's similar if they miss an easy shot, they've lost the match point ... and it is totally their fault!

Sometimes players will try to create this effect. In the French Open Final in 1999, Martina Hingis, at match point down against Steffi Graf, served an under arm first serve. She lost the match and, as the crowd judged this to be disrespectful to Graf, she was booed off the court. The crowd, however, had misunderstood the intention. I believe she did not mean to be disrespectful but did mean to create a turning point at a crucial time.

Rain breaks

Breaks in a match for rain can have a big effect on the flow of a match. They can cause a change in energy in both players which is often multiplied as time goes by. One player enjoying the fact they are still in the match and having time off court to regroup, while the other can get frustrated and worried that things might not go as well when they get on court.

Whatever the situation, the best way to approach rain breaks is to use the time well. Physically, you should change clothes, have a drink or maybe a banana, and keep warm. Mentally, you should stay focused, review your tactics and get ready to bring fresh energy to the court. If you are winning, avoid other players, with their questions and maybe distracting comments. For example, when you are 5–3 up in the final set, a well-intentioned 'Oh you should win then, who do you play next?' may not be a helpful comment!

In tennis when you get back to the court, pretend it is football. In football, long breaks for weather mean the match is abandoned and played again from the start another time. In tennis, the momentum flow having been interrupted, it may take time to be established again, so in your mind, restart the match and keep a tally of the score (starting at 0–0) from the point when you got back on court, until you feel you are back in the match.

Break and hold

To help maintain focus and distinguish between the relative importance of the passing games, and thus affect momentum, it can help to think of the score in terms of breaks and holds of serve.

This idea is based on the expectation that you should hold your serve. This is particularly true in the men's game where the serve is dominant, but it can help at any level. For example, thinking of the score in this way can make you aware that 4–1 may sound a big lead, but it may only be one break of serve. It can help you push forward to get a second break of serve if you already have one.

This way of thinking can also help you realise that a new set is a new start.

But remember – **a break is only effective if you can hold your own serve.**

Key points:

- Always try on match point down – it represents a golden opportunity.
- A new set is a new start.
- Have hope – things can always turn around.
- A combination of events often creates more of an opportunity to turn the match around.
- Don't be misled by the score – sometimes it is more useful to think of it in terms of how many *breaks and holds*.

Mental Energy: Fighting Spirit and Renewing Efforts

The key to managing momentum is linked to how much energy and focus you can bring to the match at the key times. This will be decided mainly by your desire to win the match – how great it is and why it exists in the first place. In other words, if you are playing because you really want to win, then your levels of fighting spirit are likely to be high. But even then you need to know how to respond to situations to channel your fighting spirit.

The way fighting spirit shows itself best in tennis is through clear focus and ability to renew efforts.

Focus

A player's focus, or concentration, relates to how absorbed they are in the present. The closer they are to the present, the sharper their focus. It is like imagining a torch light shining in the dark: the closer you are to the torch, the sharper the light.

Many top sports people have attributed their best ever performances to their ability to stay in the present – they often refer to it as being in the *here and now*. Poor performances, on the other hand, are often the result of a player's thoughts being distracted by past events or future possibilities. In reality, you can only improve past events or control future events by concentrating on the present.

There are many techniques to help players focus on the here and now. These are explained in detail in *The Inner Game of Tennis* (Gallwey, 1986).

Renewing efforts: why is it so important?

The trick of controlling momentum is the speed at which you renew your efforts.

If you learn to react to disappointing events (ie potential turning points) with the untypical reaction of not getting down, then you will at least be lessening the potential swing to your opponent. Don't forget that the bigger the gap between your mental energy and your opponent's, the bigger the swing in momentum.

Renewing your efforts is an individual thing. It does not necessarily mean a lot of visible bustle and bluster. In fact, immediately renewing efforts can be an internal, unemotional, professional decision.

Controlling your energy

Momentum moves quickly when one player's mental energy drops and their opponent's picks up. You cannot control your opponent's mental energy, but you should be able to control your own. How you feel inside is a kind of individual momentum and this affects the overall momentum.

It's also worth mentioning at this stage that the more there is at stake in the match, the bigger the emotional responses can be (this is why we see so many classic turning points in big events), so controlling your energy becomes more important.

This is not to say that you must be massively psyched up the whole time. It is at key moments, namely after potential turning points, when you need to increase your energy. The best players know this and get the timing of it right. This is what commentators/coaches mean when they say the best players have the ability to *go up a gear when it matters*.

What emotional level you go up from (ie your normal basic level of energy on court) is a very individual thing. Finding the right state for you on court is what is important. People are different and play well in different states of energy. Some like to bounce around the place the whole time; others prefer to be more calm and reflective until it matters. Indeed, one player I know finds that clicking his fingers makes him feel more rhythmic and energised.

You must decide how you want to be on court. Later on in this chapter there is advice for getting your mental energy level right before you go on court (see *Have your own ranking system* on page 68).

Energy on the court

Whatever basic energy levels you like to give off on court, one thing is for sure – you must avoid *copying* your opponent's energy, particularly if they are ranked higher. This is a common human trait in all walks of life. If you walk into a bar and the group you join are laughing, you follow suit. If you walk into a classroom and the feeling is one of concentration, you become focused. You should avoid copying energy on a tennis court. You will effectively end up being the *supporting actor* in the show!

You must be prepared to *set* the energy level on the court, not just react to it. This may mean being the first in the match to show really positive energy in your body language when all is quiet around you. It may mean taking your time when your opponent wants to hurry.

It may mean not dropping energy when your opponent does. This often happens when you have battled hard to establish a lead and your opponent's energy drops. The lead seems big enough so you can find yourself copying the energy level coming from the other side of the net. The problem is that your opponent may increase their energy first and you can be slow to react, still thinking, 'It'll be all right, I have a big lead'. This is what coaches mean when they say '**Don't relax if you get in front**'.

This change in energy can have a big effect on a match if it is timed to coincide with a turning point. I have even seen older players lull younger players into a false sense of security this way – they lose a few games in a set and appear to give up towards the end of the set, only to come out for the start of the next set (an ideal turning point in itself) totally fired up.

It is a cunning plan to make the energy levels on court drop when you are losing. It's called *letting the match go flat*. It suits the person who is behind, because if they were losing when the energy was high, they can't do any worse when it goes flat. (In football they do this by keeping possession in midfield.) They then wait until a key time approaches and raise their energy levels quickly to catch the opponent napping. It is a bit like being behind in a running race and shouting 'stop' and slowing down, then as the opponent begins to slow down, shouting 'go' and overtaking them.

Controlling energy and the effect of body language

How you feel inside is reflected in your body language. Good body language in between points is generally considered to involve a positive walk, a strong look, chin up, shoulders back with the racket held with the racket head up. Poor body language is generally considered to be the opposite (eg drooping shoulders and head, slow walk, negative self-talk).

Body language plays a big part in controlling the energy on court. It affects both your energy and your opponent's energy.

Your own energy is affected by your body language because you tend to feel the way you act. With clothes, when you look good you feel good, and vice versa. With friends, if you hang around with low, negative energy people, you get depressed, and vice versa. It's the same with body language: if you act as if you have low, negative energy, then you will probably make matters worse. High energy is what you want, preferably positive energy.

Body language also affects your opponent. Seeing poor body language can be a great boost to a player. Your opponent may not believe in their strength, but they will be encouraged by any signs of your weakness. Alternatively, seeing strong body language may cause your opponent to have doubts about whether they can beat you with no help from you.

Body language and juniors

Body language often reflects what players are feeling inside and their levels of mental energy, but this is not always the case. The body language of players on court can vary depending on whether or not they know their opponent.

In junior national tennis, where players nearly always know their opponent, the accepted ranking order can affect things. The underlying power of these ranking orders at national level blurs the importance of body language. For example, a better player, when threatened with aggressive body language from a player lower in the ranking order, may respond with a disinterested look. A hint to their opponent to remember their place!

However, if you are playing abroad, you may not know your opponent – they could be a club player playing well or the country's brightest young hope. Body language, therefore, becomes very important at international level, because the only information an opponent may have about you is the information you give. If you look good technically, tactically and physically, their only hope is that you have mental weaknesses.

If you look calm and in control while your opponent plays their best tennis, it gives them the message that they have to keep up that level all the way to the winning post. It suggests that you will be ready to pounce as soon as they drop their level and this in itself can raise doubts in their mind.

Keep your body language positive

It is also extremely important for juniors to invest time and effort in practising positive body language at all times so that it becomes habit. At senior level, tactics, technique and fitness tend to have equalled themselves out, and matches are won and lost more on who is the tougher player on the day.

Sharp international competitors watch their opponents and pick up signals of their mental energy in body language. If they pick up signals that you think the wheels are about to come off your performance, the only conclusion they can draw is that you are afraid it will happen – that you have a habit of falling apart. This will be the case particularly if the negative vibes have a *here we go again* feel. This only encourages your opponent.

There are two simple lessons to be learned from this:

1   If you want to succeed at a higher level, learn to control your body language. There are plenty of tricks/tools from the sports psychologists on how to do this. In simplest terms, **don't let your energy drop visibly between points.**

2   Watch the body language of your opponent and remember to keep doing it. This is easy in boxing because you are only a few feet away; in tennis you have to look closely and regularly if you want to pick up any signals. Many turning points will occur in the mind of your opponent. You may not know what causes them, but you can sense them if you keep an eye on how they're feeling. The key is to watch them regularly and not just after really obvious potential turning points.

But a word of warning: opponents can sometimes put on an act. Look out for this and be particularly sceptical if their body language is a bit too contrived – lulling players into a sense of false security is an old trick!

Key points:

- Keep your focus in the present.
- Renew your efforts quickly after a setback.
- Learn to control your energy – find another gear when it really matters.
- Set your own energy levels – don't copy your opponent's.
- Keep your body language positive.
- Keep a look out for negative signs from your opponent but beware of the *fakers*.

Tactics

Through fighting spirit and renewing your efforts, you will become a tough competitor in the heat of the battle. However, you have to make sure you are fighting the right battle. You might be fighting a battle superbly, **but it could be the wrong battle!**

Playing the right tactics at the right time can make the difference between a 5–5 battle and a 6–2 win. But what are the right tactics and when is the right time?

The right tactics

There are of course many different tactics that are right for different people on different occasions. Some general principles will help to make things clearer.

Tactics fall into two types:

* *Tactics that don't take into account the opposition.*

* *Tactics that take into account the opposition.*

Tactics that don't take into account the opposition

Before you can impose your own game you have to know what your own game is.

To help you decide, imagine how your perfect rally would look, a rally that you feel you could repeat. What would you do on the first shot of each rally? What would you want to do on the first serve and the next shot, the second serve and the next shot? Think about the same thing on the returns of serve. If you were in a rally, how would you want it to end?

By doing this you will come up with a *basic plot* for your tennis.

Basic plot tennis is playing the game with which you are familiar in as solid and consistent a way as possible. It is your style. Baseline tennis for a natural baseliner is basic plot tennis. Basic plot tennis for a natural serve and volleyer is serve and volley tennis. It is playing your own game and involves knowing your favourite patterns of play.

One-off tennis is when you do something that departs from the basic plot. It is different from the way you usually play and has probably caught your opponent unawares. One-offs are of course less reliable than basic plots and may not come off. But when they do they can interrupt the flow of a match and may alter it significantly.

In order to manage momentum, it is important to understand the differences between basic plot and one-off tennis. There are times when you need to revert to one style or the other. For example, if you are in a tie-break and your opponent is nervous, making a basic plot point would be the right decision.

However, imagine you had held a 5–2 lead but were now in a tie-break, having lost the lead and with the match flow going against you. Trying to win the tie-break against the flow (or *run of play*) may well demand coming up with something different – which might mean a one-off, or several, to snatch the set and therefore the momentum.

On the other hand, if you were 1–4 and had come back to win the set by playing one-off tennis because you had nothing to lose, then at the start of the next set you may need to return to basic plot tennis. You may not be able to rely on a rich vein of one-off tennis now the *nothing to lose* feeling has gone.

Understanding the differences between basic plot and one-off tennis allows you to guess the likely future and get some perspective on what the score is telling you. If you have lost a close set but missed a few one-offs you shouldn't have gone for, while your opponent has made some they wouldn't normally make, then you could have cause to be optimistic. If the reverse is true, you shouldn't rest on your laurels.

The person who controls the basic plot in a match very often dictates with whom the underlying momentum lies. Seeing who controls the basic plot points of a match can be done more easily from a distance. At the LTA Indoor Masters, I once had to watch several important matches at once and so watched the furthest only intermittently:

- At 2–3 I could see the mother of the girl who was losing looking very tense and pacing the balcony above the court. However, from a distance I could also tell she actually had nothing to worry about. Her daughter was playing closer to the baseline, was calmer and was continually creating opportunities she was just missing. On the other hand, her daughter's opponent was stressed, making impressive shots she couldn't keep on making and was benefiting from a few lucky net cords. In fact, her daughter was controlling the basic plot tennis, and went on to win 6–4, 6–3.

Changeovers can provide a good opportunity to analyse whether or not you should change tactics to create a change in momentum. Imagine you are watching your own match from a distance – what would your general impressions be? Are you controlling the basic plot points?

Being able to analyse who is controlling the basic plot like this can also help you mentally. It is important not to panic if things don't go your way immediately. If you know you are controlling the basic plot, you can stay calm. If you just react to the score, panic and rush to hit winners to get back into the match, you are more likely to lose momentum quickly. I remember an example of this with one of my players:

- Sarah was once 2–4 in the semi-finals of the national 14U Championships. At that point, she was actually controlling the basic plot rallies but had lost some crucial points due to one-off happenings and so was behind in the game score. She could have dropped her energy and effort because it was an important match and things seemed to be going against her. She kept her cool, however, and went on to win the match 6–4, 6–3 and later, the tournament.

Tactics that take into account the opposition

All players have strengths and weaknesses. There are many tactics that can be used to exploit their weaknesses or at least avoid their strengths.

Individual weaknesses/strengths can be:

- **technical** (eg not liking low balls due to a strong western grip or having good angles due to hooking the ball)

- **mental** (eg never hitting a topspin backhand due to lack of confidence or being good at the net due to being aggressive)

- **tactical** (eg usually missing wide balls because of trying for a flash winner down the line every time or being tough to pass due to a good approach shot down the line)

- **physical** (eg not moving well to the left due to a bad right leg or defending well because of great speed around the court).

As well as individual strengths and weaknesses, many players play to certain styles. For example, some always hit everything at one pace – very hard; others hit everything very soft, like a spongy wall! Some players can change the pace of the ball at will; others can do so only if they are given pace to work with first. Some initiate the play, others simply react.

There are two different ways to beat these various types of players:

- **Give them what they don't like.** For example, you serve wide to a player with a strong western forehand grip, or come to the net on their backhand if they always slice it.

- **Don't allow them to be successful with their favourite basic plot plan.** This works because when their favourite shot is not getting them points, they lose hope and can't see where the points are going to come from. Similarly, when they get cheap points from their basic plot, their confidence soars. For example: keep net players away from the net; don't make silly errors against consistent players; make big servers play the next ball as often as possible by blocking the return.

There are many ways to exploit weaknesses, but sometimes concentrating on the opponent's game too much means you forget your own game. To keep things simple in the heat of the battle, you are often better off letting them worry about how to deal with your imposing game. Being the initiator of the play is crucial if you want to keep the future in your own hands and it's the first shot of the rally that often decides who takes charge of the point – the reality of high level tennis these days is **hit or be hit!**

Key points:

- Make sure you choose the right tactics – fight the right battle.
- Know your own game. What is your basic plot? When can you afford to play one-offs?
- Be aware of your opponent's strengths and weaknesses – play smarter, not harder.

Consistency

Being consistent is very important. Whether you aim to attack or defend, you need to get the ball in court.

Consistency and its effect on the flow of the match

Consistency can have a major effect on the flow of the match. If you simply do not miss and do not look as if you are going to miss, this can have a strong mental impact on your opponent. If they know that in order to beat you, they are going to have to keep their tennis above your level of consistency for a long period of time, then their confidence can drop and even a consistent player may start to make errors.

The effect is like that of an arm wrestle. If you keep the pressure on for long enough then the opponent will wilt. Some sooner, some later, depending on their mental toughness.

This is shown if you chart a match related to points won and lost in a row (see *Charting matches* on page 74). You will often see close, hard-fought periods followed by one player losing a string of quicker points, before the consistent battle continues. This often occurs after five or so games in junior international tennis.

Working on this approach is very successful and combines many of the qualities needed for higher-level tennis: self-discipline, concentration, determination, and physical fitness.

Vary your game

Equally, it is important to vary your own game, so you don't become a victim of a clever opponent. You need to vary basic plays – one in five is enough – to keep your opponent from reading your game.

The best time to vary is when you are in the lead. Your opponent won't remember that you only go for a serve wide to the forehand when you are 30–0 up, they will simply be aware that sometimes you can serve wide to the forehand.

However, you can be even cleverer.

> Greg Rusedski, for example, has a relatively poor backhand passing shot, except for a very slow cross-court one, but a great serve. He knows he can hold his serve and may get one chance to break. So, every time he gets a passing shot, he blasts them hard (and often wildly) down the line ... until he has a chance to change the flow in his direction when he goes for his cross-court, placed shot.

It works so often. Having built up one pattern, the switch can work at a crucial time.

The right time

How can these different tactics be used at the right time? Playing the right shot at the right time can make the difference between winning a tie-break and losing it. But when is the right time?

The answer is on the **big points**. A lot of talk in tennis is about the big points. Certain points are called big points because they are worth more than others: 30–30 is clearly more important than 15–15, because whoever wins the next point gets a game point. What is often missed, though, is the effect of big points at crucial stages of the match. A 30–30 point at 5–5 is usually more important than a 30–30 at 1–1, in terms of winning the set. This is because of the effect winning a set can have on the flow of the match. Big points are really points at which **a change in the flow could take place.**

Therefore the **right time** to employ your chosen tactics (and have the best mental response) is the time (or the points) when there is the **biggest chance of affecting the momentum flow.** This is obviously the case when the momentum is neutral, but could also be at the beginning of a set to change the flow in your favour.

You can employ tactics, of course, at any time, but beware – if your opponent has the flow with them, your tactics may not be as effective.

The player who your coach promised would never topspin their passing shots cross-court, may well do nothing else when the flow is with them! (I have to admit I made promises like that before I realised the momentum flow implications.) Things will, however, be different when the momentum is neutral. For example, the topspin passing shots of this player may just hit the top of the net or land in the tramlines as a result of the player feeling more under pressure.

Key points:

- Get the ball in the court – consistency matters.
- Keep your opponent guessing.
- Learn to play the right shot at the right time.

Preparation

Preparing for a match: any match

Warming up means preparing so that there are *no surprises* when the match begins and you can get off to a good start.

To help them prepare well, many good players hit for about half an hour, one or two hours before they play. Careful planning can ensure this final practice is effective:

- If possible, make sure you hit on the court you will play on, or at least the same surface, to ensure there are no surprises linked to court surround, for example.
- Warm up your muscles by running, stretching and hitting the ball, to ensure your muscles get no surprises and you remain injury free.
- Try to feel what you are likely to experience when the match begins, to ensure that there are no surprises mentally when you start play (eg imagine the presence of an umpire, a crowd, hitting your serve on the first point of the game).

It may be that things are not as you wish during the hit. At least, though, you will have time before your match to come up with some answers rather than having to deal with this problem during the match itself. Do not, however, fall into the common trap of wanting everything to go perfectly in practice before a match. It won't all go perfectly in the match so don't demand that it does in practice. **The point of the practice is to prepare for getting things right during the match.**

If you cannot hit before your match then at least warm up your muscles, and try to get in touch with how you feel and will want to feel, before you play, even if it's only in the changing room.

Finally, preparing for no surprises does not guarantee you won't get any! You almost certainly will. Think of how many perfect matches you have ever played? So when things go wrong, remember: **it's not what goes wrong, but your reaction to what goes wrong that matters.**

Preparing for a match: specific matches

What makes tennis unpredictable is that tennis players do not always perform like machines to a certain level. Players play better some days and worse others. It often depends on their mental energy going into the match.

It is not uncommon to see matches in which players *roll over* for opponents they consider to be better. It is also not uncommon to see the same player fighting as if their life depended on it in order to beat a lower-ranked player. In the first case they give too much respect to the higher-ranked player, while in the second they fight harder than ever against the lower-ranked player because **there are some people you just don't lose to.**

In both situations there is an underlying current of feeling that affects how the players play. To a large degree it is produced by ranking systems which are external to the player, such as national ratings, club ratings, seedings, world rankings, and so on. It is important therefore to have a ranking system that is individual to you and that helps you view each match in the best possible way for you. So, don't rely on a ranking system someone else has produced.

Have your own ranking system

If a ranking system is going to work it has to be based on tennis expertise, on an understanding of how tennis works, rather than simply on previous results. Using that understanding it is possible to produce a scheme in which players fall into one of four categories:

1   Very much worse than you *(one-star match)*

2   A little bit worse than you *(two-star match)*

3   A little bit better than you *(three-star match)*

4   Very much better than you *(four-star match)*

In theory, you could have an extra category for players who are the same, but in reality someone is nearly always the favourite.

This ranking system has psychological implications and is a system that can help you understand in advance how momentum might be managed in the matches.

One-star and four-star matches are relatively straightforward to handle mentally. This is because you know what will happen and the human mind is at its happiest when the situation is predictable. Humans find unpredictable situations more scary (eg dark alleys, spiders, snakes)!

In other words, if you are playing a player who is very much better than you (four-star match) then you have little to lose, and everyone knows you have little to lose. If for example, you are playing the number one seed in a major tournament, then in one sense you can't lose. If you get a good score everyone will say 'well done – you'll beat them next time' or 'you're coming along really well'. And if you lose heavily then it is no more than everyone expected. If you win, you get rewarded with ranking points, publicity and possibly prize money.

If your opponent is very much worse than you (one-star match), then it is often a case of you settling your nerves as soon as you can, remaining focused and cruising to a victory with relaxed tennis.

It is the second and third categories that provide particular challenges. In the case of the two-star and three-star matches you do not really know what will happen.

Two-star matches can be particularly testing. Not only are they unpredictable, but your opponent is likely to be *hunting* you. It is not easy to play matches when you know you are being hunted.

If you do come through these uncomfortable feelings and win, the result will be no more than was expected. Even before the match you may have people asking you who you are playing in the following match. Yet we should not forget that to win a tournament as a seeded player, even a Grand Slam tournament such as Wimbledon or the US Open, you have to win a large number of two-star matches. Number one seeds, in particular, have to win a large number of two-star matches and have learned how to do so.

Three-star matches are also tough. But this time you are hunting them, and it is normally a little bit easier to be the hunter rather than the hunted. You still cannot easily predict what will happen, but it is challenging and you know that your opponent will probably be feeling more uncomfortable about the match than you. But, as with a two-star match, you are still in unknown territory and you have to deal with the unknown.

At least, in two-star and three-star matches (as with all matches) you have approximately 40–90 minutes to work out what is going on, to solve problems and come successfully through the match. But you walk onto the court not knowing what is going to happen. The most successful players are those who learn to enjoy the challenge of the unknown.

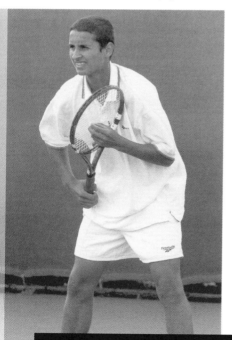

It is also very important to make your own assessment of two-star and three-star wins. For example, if you have not played for three weeks because of injury and are entering a tournament with a heavy cold, your first match, according to the external ranking system, may be a one-star match. But for you at that particular point it is a two-star match. You will get no credit for winning it, but, if you do, you will know it was a good win. Similarly for female players, pre-menstrual syndrome (PMS) may affect what assessment they make for a match.

Another example of a three-star win is where you win a match you are expected to win (that is, a two-star match) when your form is poor. By your standards it is a three-star win, even if the rankings tell a different story.

It's not what goes wrong but your reaction to what goes wrong that matters

By learning to get your mind right before you play, you can begin to manage momentum before the match. Because they involve dealing with the unknown and unpredictable, the two-star and three-star matches are trickier than the one-star and four-star matches. While all matches are important, the significance of the two-star ones is often underestimated.

The two-star matches are the most difficult of all, because seemingly you have nothing to win. Be a tennis expert – know that all tennis players find it tough to play well in these matches. For this reason, make the two-star matches the ones to get psyched up for. After all, if you win all these matches, you will always have a good season.

When Jimmy Connors, arguably one of the toughest competitors ever, was interviewed before a match he was expected to win and asked about the outcome, he would usually say something like:

I don't predict matches. I really don't know if I'm going to win. But I do know one thing. If the other guy's going to win he'll have one hell of a fight on his hands. He'll have to work really hard.

This is an excellent attitude to approaching the unknown.

Key points:

- The point of the practice is to prepare for getting things right during the match.

- It's not what goes wrong but your reaction to what goes wrong that matters.

- Employ your own ranking system. Prepare yourself to do the hunting or to be hunted.

- Think of the unknown as a challenge, not a threat.

- Think of some of your opponents – in what category would you place them?

- Go through the five stages of momentum – imagine what each of these opponents would be like in each of the five stages.

Chapter Four

Momentum and the Wider Picture

Momentum and Coaching: What's the Link?

Most tennis coaching concentrates on improving the general tennis standard of the player. Tennis coaches often talk about factors relating to the overall standard of tennis that is being played. They talk about statistics, for example: percentage of first serves, attacking short balls, body language, unforced errors.

This is clearly very important because your tennis skills have a big influence on momentum. Your range and ability of skills is your weaponry when going into battle. For example, if you only have tennis shots equivalent to some rusty tanks while your opponent has new tanks and an air force, then the impact of controlling the momentum will have much less effect.

Knowing what your normal playing level is will help you know what is and isn't acceptable at your level. This awareness will drive you on in a match to play to your standard. No matter where the momentum lies, if you know what your standard is and work to achieve it, you will probably be better off in the match.

So working on improving your standard is important, but it is not the whole picture. Whatever standard you achieve, when standards are close, battles take place which require knowledge of battle skills involving momentum flow. The importance of these skills is in danger of getting lost in today's high-tech world of sports science based coaching.

For instance, it doesn't matter how brilliant your serve becomes technically, if you cannot produce first serves at the right time, you will never be a great match player.

The overriding views in the coaching world today seem to focus on applying all the skills all the time, mainly to improve general standards for the reasons outlined above. For example, most of the mental coaching revolves around getting players to concentrate the whole time. Even sports psychologists seem to spend nearly all their time designing tools on how to improve specific mental skills (eg concentration, attitude, motivation), seemingly without paying much attention to when to use them at different times in a match.

In my experience, what players really want to know is why they just lost the battle they had been involved in and perhaps very nearly won, as well as general ideas to improve their overall standard.

Young tennis players in particular, see specific shots at specific times as more important. They struggle to relate to the fact that less unforced errors over a period of time will pay off, especially when they notice that Henman makes some of the worst you've seen but hits two great shots at a crucial time, and still wins; that Hingis doesn't show a strong image all the time; and that Rusedski can have a low percentage of first serves, then hit four aces in a tie-break to win the set.

Here are some examples you may have heard:

- *When you are going through a bad patch, just stick at it and it could all turn round*
- *Don't relax and let the other player back into the match*
- *Be alert and take advantage of the period when your opponent might relax*
- *Hit a big one and it can turn the game around*
- *Always play the percentage shot on the big points*
- *If your opponent is playing well ... weather the storm*
- *Mix it up to break up their rhythm*
- *If things aren't going well, slow the game down*

The trick is that they do it when it matters by knowing when it matters.

Knowing when it matters allows players to use their skills more decisively and with pinpoint accuracy. It's like teaching players to be snipers rather than brainless knuckleheads with machine guns!

The strange thing about momentum is that although everyone talks about it in one form or another, very little has been written about it. Coaching books are full of one-off references to it and coaches do talk about it, but not in a structured way.

Each of the above is good advice, but the problem is that it is difficult to apply. It can be useful **after** a match to think about these things, but how do you bring it all together **during** a match?

The basis of all these statements is in momentum flow. Read through the phrases again, thinking about the five stages of momentum and you will see how they can make sense.

In order to teach players about momentum, the most important thing is to get them to watch matches, to talk about examples of turning points, how they came about and what reaction each player had to them.

Coaches can discuss with their players how each player reacts in each of the stages (eg when their backs are up against the wall, when they are in control and when things are hanging in the balance). It is particularly important to explain the opportunities created by the score at various points (eg the start of sets, big points, being match point down) and how your attitude can help or hinder at these crucial times.

Improve your players' 'match-craft', not just their skills

Charting matches

Charting matches in a statistical way doesn't always show the whole picture. Yet this is still the main way that matches are charted.

It makes sense to aim for the higher percentage of first serves in, but how can a player believe this when they know that a couple of aces at key times can win matches even if none of their other first serves go in. An ace at 5–5 30–30 is worth a lot, and this isn't shown in statistics.

How can it make sense to a player who is told 'you missed too many returns', when they know that just one return, on break point at 4–3, would have won them the match. In other words, if that return alone had gone in, then the momentum flow would have been on their side. They would then have been much more relaxed, and consequently the returns might have gone in and the statistics would have been different.

For statistics to become meaningful for a player, they need to be calculated with the five stages of momentum in mind as opposed to an overall total. This would make match charting much more revealing.

My preferred method is to use a piece of graph paper and, starting at the centre line, mark a dot each time a point is won or lost (see graph on facing page). Mark the dot one square of graph paper up for each time your player wins the point and one dot down for each time a point is lost. Continue the pattern until the end of each set, marking down the game score and who is serving as the match continues.

This method allows the flow of points to be seen but can also be used to identify (or circle) certain key points or events. You may need to jot down a note so you can remember the point. For example, it is often very interesting to note a player's reaction to a potential turning point. More symbols can be added, according to the information desired (see graph). You can design your own key.

Going through the graph after the match allows a player to learn more about the flow of the match and analyse their responses to certain situations.

Sarah vs Helen 16U National Champs Final 2nd Set

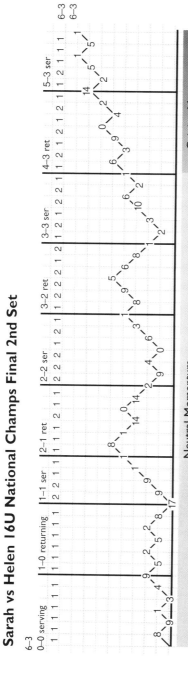
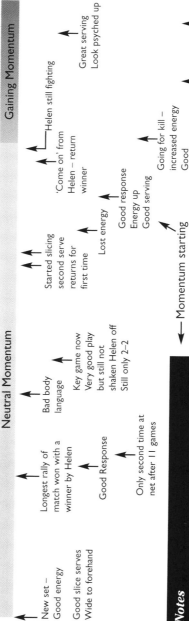

Neutral Momentum

Gaining Momentum

Momentum starting to go against you →

New set – Good energy

Good slice serves Wide to forehand

Longest rally of match won with a winner by Helen

Good Response

Only second time at net after 11 games

Bad body language

Key game now Very good play but still not shaken Helen off Still only 2–2

Started slicing second serve returns for first time

Lost energy

Good response Energy up Good serving

'Come on' from Helen – return winner

Helen still fighting

Going for kill – increased energy Good

Great serving Look psyched up

Net cord

Net cord

Notes

- Comments relate to Sarah unless stated
- Top line gives the game score
- Second line down indicates whether it was a first (1) or second (2) serve
- Numbers on chart itself relate to the length of the rally.

Key points:

- Good coaches will improve their players' skills. Excellent coaches will help their players to play *smart* tennis when it really matters.

- Statistics are more useful to players if they are put in context with the flow of the match.

Momentum and Sport

Why do people who like one sport tend to be interested in sport in general? Why is competing so interesting? After all, every sport is different. Here are some of the differences:

- **Scoring systems** – some sports have systems based on *definites*, such as scoring a goal; others, like gymnastics, are based on performance.

- **Time periods** – sports, such as football, involve playing for ninety minutes; others, such as cricket matches, can take up to five days to complete.

- **Number of players** – this can vary from up to 80 in American football to just two in tennis.

- **Competitive formats** – most involve *head-to-head* or *team-to-team* competition but some, such as golf, do not.

- **Length of time/space for possession of the ball** – in some sports you must pass the ball within a certain time; some sports allow contact while others do not.

So what is it that links these different sports together? The answer is that although sports may appear to have different frameworks, rules etc, **momentum links them all.** Swings in momentum, turning points, comebacks, upsets are common to them all. It is these that make up the flow of momentum in a match; and it is the flow of momentum and competitors' human reactions to it that fascinates people, not necessarily just their skills.

In 1999, there were two great examples of momentum changing the *wheels of fortune:*

- The European Cup final between Manchester United and Bayern Munich was a classic. It was Manchester United's big focus for the season and it was meant to be their day. The expectation was massive. However, the match didn't go as planned. Bayern Munich went 1–0 up and held onto their lead as the clock ticked. Nothing seemed to be going right for United, there were no flowing moves and players seemed to have heavy legs. It looked at if it wasn't going to be their day.

Momentum is a powerful force experienced by players from all sports

Then, as time ran out, two crucial turning points happened. Firstly Bayern Munich hit the post. It could have been 2–0 and game over. Then, minutes later Bayern attacked again, the Bayern striker got through the defence, and chipped Schmichel, the United goalkeeper. Schmichel, a big man, stood rooted to the spot and could only watch as the ball floated over his head and headed towards the empty goal. It was too good, beating such a big guy with a quality chip. Only it wasn't to be, the ball hit the cross bar and bounced away harmlessly. In that moment the whole match turned. The energy of both teams changed. It could have been 2–0 or even 3–0. In fact it probably should have been. But it wasn't, it was still 1–0.

Suddenly to the United players, 1–0 which had been a disastrous score line all night, suddenly seemed like a *god-given* gift. Their energy levels soared. When Bayern saw this change in energy, they froze. You could see their thoughts, this was unfair and now huge fears about the final few minutes dawned on them.

A bigger swing in momentum has rarely been seen, the energy of both teams changing together, mirrored back to the players and increased by the reaction of both sets of supporters. With hardly any time left, Manchester United went straight on the attack and scored. Then within a minute and now into injury time they won a corner. The Bayern players were totally distraught with their minds jumping both into the past with distress at what had happened and into the future with fear. You could sense what was going to happen.

The corner came across, Solskjaer reacted first and Manchester United won the match 2–1. Possibly the most dramatic end to a football match all century, right at the end of it!

- Another example of how momentum changed the course of an event, happened in the 1999 Ryder Cup between Europe and the United States. After two days' play and with only the singles matches left to play, Europe led by ten matches to six. The Ryder Cup was effectively won by a decision the American Captain made that evening.

Realising that his team needed to build momentum early on, he placed all his best players to go first in the order so by the time the crucial later matches came on, his lesser players would be playing with a building momentum in the overall match score to push them on. (Normally he would have saved his top players, so they would be last on the course when the score got close at the end.)

The plan worked to perfection and at 10–10 the match was anything but even, with the American crowd roaring on their players. At the end the American team was so psyched up by the surge of energy, that things nearly got out of hand, but they came back to snatch a dramatic victory from the Europeans.

Audience effects

Momentum exists in all sports, the same patterns exist and the same approaches apply. You can see this clearly by examining the crowds that watch sport.

Sporting crowds have a real feel for the flow of momentum. Football crowds are particularly well-tuned into momentum; they care passionately who wins and can often feel when their team is likely to score or concede a goal. You can almost always tell how well a team is doing by listening to a crowd or looking at the expressions on their faces.

Even more interestingly, the fans act as a mirror, reflecting back the energy of the team and therefore adding to it, either making things better or worse. For example, if the team is nervous, the fans get nervous, which makes the team more nervous, and so on.

The importance of raising energy to create a change in the momentum was discussed earlier on in this book. Crowds can provide energy for their team or player through support. This is why it is an advantage to play at home. It is also why you can see such dramatic momentum swings when the crowds are at their loudest and believe anything can happen, typically in FA Cup matches.

In tennis there have been examples of crowds influencing the flow of a match. They can contribute towards the combination effect if, for instance, you stand up for your rights and the crowd *boos* you thinking you are time-wasting. Jimmy Connors, on the other hand, appeared to be very good at using the crowd to maintain his momentum or more often disrupt his opponent's.

Crowds can influence the flow of a match

Key points:

- Momentum links all sports together.

- Understanding the flow of momentum in other sports and how the best sportspeople deal with this can improve your tennis.

- Be aware of the effect of an audience – make it your friend, not your foe!

The Hidden Force in Sport and Life

The patterns of momentum flow can be seen on different scales. You can see turning points take place in a rally, a match, a season and even over the course of a tennis player's career.

> A key turning point in Ivan Lendl's career was when he won his first Grand Slam final in the French Open final after being two sets to love down against John McEnroe. Until that point he had lost several Grand Slam finals and people were saying he hadn't got what it takes. After that match he amassed enough Grand Slam titles to put him on a level with some of the all time great players.

Momentum and form

Over the course of a season, a player's form sometimes has momentum with it, or against, or appears to be neutral. Form too, can be found in each of the five stages of momentum.

What is more, much of the same advice applies. For example, when a player's form is going through a good patch (ie it has the momentum with it), it is important to know ***how it got there*** so it can be repeated or extended. For example, has it come after a period of practice or a lot of matches won easily, or a period of playing on the same surface or a period of rest?

If your form has improved from 7/10 to 10/10 by working hard on the basics, then remember that. If your form loses momentum, don't expect 10/10 to come just because you can remember the feeling of 10/10 and want to achieve it. Put in the necessary work/planning.

Here are some fundamental principles to help you respond in the best way to the ebbs and flows of your form:

- If things are going really well, ***step up a gear*** – play with better players, enter some tournaments of a higher standard than usual.

- If your form seems neutral, ***don't wait*** – go and take the initiative. For example, you may need extra practice, more fitness work, extra coaching, or to improve your concentration.

- If you are off-form, **don't lose hope** – be positive about the fact that things will get better and work out what you need to do. On a bigger scale, do you need to develop your overall game tactics or just be better at the ones you have? Choose your tournaments carefully and take one match at a time. The road back to good form will seem steep, but as always, it gets less steep when you start to get things right.

Momentum and flow in life

Momentum is fact beyond sport, it is with us in life itself. The patterns of momentum flow can be seen throughout all aspects of life: business careers, relationships, or simply how your day is going.

On a small scale, a good or bad phone call (even about a minor thing) can change your day, depending on your response to it, in the same way that getting a new job can change your life on a bigger scale. Momentum in life is referred to on a regular basis – for example the manager of a stockbrokers on Wall Street recently criticised his day traders for following the momentum, not changing it.

Many phrases are linked to the flow of momentum in life, and the parallels with tennis are obvious:

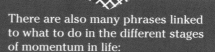

- *Down in the doldrums*
- *Things are in the balance*
- *Pride comes before a fall*
- *Going through a bad patch*
- *Plain sailing*
- *The tide has turned*
- *The darkest hour is just before dawn*
- *On a roll*
- *There's light at the end of the tunnel*

There are also many phrases linked to what to do in the different stages of momentum in life:

- *Nose to the grindstone*
- *Don't count your chickens*
- *Knuckle down*
- *Cheer up – worse things happen at sea*
- *Make hay while the sun shines*
- *Take the bull by the horns*
- *Chin up*
- *He who hesitates is lost*

Perhaps one difference between tennis and life is that in life you don't always have to compete with just one person all the time. Life is like riding a wave as a surfer, responding to external factors ... tennis competition is like surfing alongside someone else, with both surfers responding to the external factors but also both trying to push each other off!

Either way, there are many similarities between life and sport, and many of the responses used in tennis can also be used to deal with what life throws at you.

For example, if things are going well on a day-to-day basis, then good things seem to just happen. Pieces of good news seem to come quickly and because you feel good, the positive energy in you seems to attract positive behaviour from people around. In tennis, you'd need to be aware of relaxing your guard too much. It's the same in day-to-day life, if things are going well at work, you still need to guard against being too arrogant so things don't turn against you. For instance, if you'd gone for an interview for promotion at work, you would be unwise to go around telling everyone you felt confident you'd got it because the interview went well, before you had heard officially. The same phrases apply in sport and life in this situation, such as *Don't count your chickens* or *Don't tempt fate.*

On the other hand, when things are going against you, bad news seems to land on your doorstep all the time. Sometimes when you are on a downward slide, things can seem to go from bad to worse. As in tennis, you need to take your time and not make any rash decisions. At times, you may need to bite your lip and walk away from certain situations. Your attitude is the key – keep positive and you will have a better chance of things turning around. *The darkest hour is just before the dawn.*

There are also times when life just seems to tick by. It can be tempting to sit back and wait for something to happen but this is often a good time to be proactive and shift the momentum in your favour. Hence the phrase – *take the bull by the horns.* Depending on the situation, this might mean going on a training course, taking a holiday or changing jobs.

There are clearly many parallels between momentum flow in tennis and momentum flow in other sports. Sport reflects life. Life reflects sport. Or more accurately **they both reflect patterns of momentum.**

Key points:

- Learn from other sports.
- Momentum exists on different scales.
- Managing momentum flow can be transferred from tennis to life and vice versa.

Conclusion

The art of competing

The best players at any level are aware of how to react at various stages of a match. They know the landmarks and are able to sense any potential shifts in momentum. This allows them to apply the correct tactics at the correct time, and seemingly to step up a gear when it matters.

While some players have this knowledge instinctively, most players acquire it through years of experience. Anyone can learn it. The key is to recognise the important points in matches and respond with the correct attitude and tactics. Many potential turning points can be predicted but others become apparent during the course of the match. It is possible to get your reaction right at the time, as long as you know what is required and your attitude is right (*Chapters 2 and 3*). As with all learning processes, initially you are aware of it consciously but eventually it becomes second nature.

This approach is more advanced than simply trying very hard in the same way on every point. From time to time, you need to be aware of the bigger picture, before refocusing on the present again. If you only focus on the present without standing back and taking the momentum flow into account, you can be caught unawares. It is like having a video camera with a zoom lens that is constantly *zoomed in* – without zooming out occasionally – you might not be ready for something important which is about to come into shot.

There are, in addition, some advantages of this approach: you will save mental and physical energy because you know the times to really focus all your efforts; you will benefit from the mental change of pace that gives you some variety and therefore helps you to go on longer; and you will benefit from the effect a mental change of pace can have on your opponent – playing someone who steps up a gear mentally at the right time can be very frustrating.

By understanding the different stages of momentum, you will learn to apply all you know about your opponent's weaknesses at key times. It will also help you achieve a high level of focus more easily for longer periods and know why you should never give up. It will enable you to see and control this hidden force. You will become a mentally tough competitor; learn to win the war of a tennis match even if you lose some battles along the way, and begin to master the art of competing.

Golden rules

No theories and stories are worth much without practical application. If you remember nothing else from this book, remember the following:

- *A new set is a new start.*
- *Be prepared to work hard when you are close to winning.*
- *Don't copy the energy of your opponent, do what you want to do.*
- *Get the ball in the court – consistency matters.*
- *It's not what goes wrong that matters, it's your reaction to it.*
- *Have hope – things can always turn around.*
- *Always try on match point down, it represents a golden opportunity.*
- *Keep an eye on what your opponent's body language tells you.*
- *Be positive about outside distractions; the more distractions, the greater chance that your opponent will be distracted.*
- *Renew your efforts quickly – the trick of controlling momentum is the speed at which you renew your efforts.*
- *Fighting spirit is not only needed when you are behind.*
- *The point of the practice is to prepare for getting things right during the match.*
- *Play smarter, not harder.*
- *Managing momentum flow can be transferred from tennis to life and vice versa.*

Enough talk about mental toughness and battle skills. Now, over to you! When is your next battle?